ROVER'S REBIRTH

The Post-War Renaissance

1945–1953

ROVER'S REBIRTH

The Post-War Renaissance
1945–1953

JAMES TAYLOR

THE CROWOOD PRESS

The
LAND-ROVER
FIRE ENGINE

Contents

Introduction

When peace returned to Britain at the end of World War II in 1945, Britain's car manufacturers were faced with the task of getting back into their traditional business after six years of focusing on producing war matériel. It was not easy and, for Rover, was complicated by the decision to move into a new factory some fifteen miles west of their old one.

The first job was to get back into making cars, and only after that was there time to develop new designs. For Rover, the process of creating a new model that met their standards was a long and difficult one, complicated by the government's insistence that they should prioritise models that would sell well outside Britain. For a small company that had never given much thought to exports before, this was a very tall order.

Yet in these difficult times, Rover fell back on the combination of sound business management and engineering expertise that had helped it avoid collapse in the early 1930s. In fact, the pressure of those difficult times led to a new tradition for Rover, of having far more new ideas than they could reasonably put into production. Many of them were innovative, and would go on to give the company a unique and much respected position within the British motor industry in the two decades after the war.

Studies of Rover's products in that period have tended to focus on individual types, such as the P4 saloons or the Land-Rover. This approach unavoidably minimises the interdependency of the company's products, which played an important part in their remarkable renaissance. The critical period in the post-war era was the years 1945–1953, and it is this period and its products that this book covers. In 1945 Rover was really starting from almost nothing, and by 1953 they were once again on a sound footing and were looking at further expansion.

James Taylor
Oxfordshire
November 2023

Timeline

1944 First work on proposed new post-war Model M.

1945 Work recommences on IOE engines and box-section chassis planned before the war.
Rover moves into Solihull factory. Production of lightly revised pre-war cars begins.

1946 Design work on new bodies runs into difficulties. First Model M prototypes. Re-orientation of design work now aims for an interim model (P3) and a second more modern model (P4).

1947 Model M abandoned in favour of Land-Rover. Studebakers obtained from USA to assist P4 development.

1948 P3 saloons replace revised pre-war types (February). Land-Rover introduced (April). First overseas assembly operations begin.

1949 P4 saloons replace P3 models.
100bhp gas turbine engine runs. Land-Rover production and sales exceed those of Rover cars.

1950 Demonstration runs of first gas turbine car prototype (JET 1).

1951 First work on a more conventional gas turbine car. First work on Road-Rover project.

1952 JET 1 sets a record 152mph (245km/h) at Jabbeke. New share issue brings in finance for major expansion plans.

1953 Gas turbine department becomes Rover Gas Turbines Ltd. First work on new smaller Rover saloon with V6 engine. Rover introduce four new models: 60 and 90 saloons, and 86 and 107 Land-Rovers.

CHAPTER 1

Background and Overview

By the time World War II began in September 1939, the Rover Company enjoyed a solid reputation in Britain as the makers of 'One of Britain's Fine Cars'. The slogan dated from 1936, by which time the company had emerged from a difficult financial period in the early years of the decade and had begun to earn the lasting respect of the professional classes for whom its cars were mostly built.

Rover in this period was based in Coventry, with its main factory and headquarters at Helen Street in the Stoke Heath (now Foleshill) district to the northeast of the city centre. It had an exceptionally strong management team, with the board of directors led by Ransom Harrison, Howe Graham as financial director, and S. B. (Spencer) Wilks as managing director. Chief engineer was Maurice Wilks, the younger brother of the managing director, and he oversaw an equally strong team of engineers. Rover was an independent company, quite small by motor industry standards, but it was run almost like a family business and engendered great loyalty from its employees. By the end of the 1930s, it was selling between 10,000 and 11,000 cars a year.

World War II brought this idyllic existence to an abrupt end. Rover introduced their 1940-model cars as planned in September 1939, but had already turned part of their manufacturing capability over to repairing military aircraft. Since the middle of the decade, they had been running a 'shadow factory' at Acocks Green, building

S. B. Wilks was the level-headed managing director on whose guidance the Rover Company depended heavily.

Maurice Wilks was the enthusiastic and innovative driving force behind Rover engineering.

aero engines for military use, and during 1939 they took on the management of a second one, at Solihull to the southeast of Birmingham. Car production was halted on government orders in May 1940, and the entire resources of the company were redirected to the war effort. The Helen Street factory was severely damaged by enemy bombing in the Coventry Blitz in November 1940, and the Rover staff dispersed – some of them to a group of repurposed cotton mills in Lancashire and Yorkshire, where they assisted Frank Whittle with the development of his jet engine for aircraft.

It was not until June 1944, as the D-Day landings made clear that the tide of war in Europe was turning, that Rover was able to contemplate with any clarity its future as a car manufacturer. No new design work had been done during the war years, although new models had been planned before the war and the work done for them had not been lost. The Helen Street factory in

This poor-quality photograph is the only known picture of the Rover Board as it was in 1945. In the centre is Ransom Harrison, the chairman. On the left are George Farmer (assistant secretary and chief accountant), Frank Ward (secretary) and S. B. Wilks (managing director). On the right are Howe Graham (vice-chairman) and Sir Geoffrey Savage (works director).

Coventry had been hastily patched up to enable it to continue producing war matériel, but there was a tantalising alternative to returning there. The Solihull factory was much newer, more modern, and larger, and the government had offered Rover first refusal on it once it was no longer needed for war work.

Rover's initial offer to buy the factory outright was rejected, but subsequent discussions about a long-term lease proved fruitful. In February 1945, the Rover Board agreed to lease the factory and to dispose of the Helen Street works, which was sold in July to the Coventry machine tool makers Alfred Herbert. By March, Rover had begun to move into their new Solihull headquarters.

A New Dawn

As early as 1944, the company had also begun to think about the cars it would be selling once peace returned. There were still many unknowns, of course, and whatever plans they developed would have to be modified in the light of events. No surviving documents tell us who took the responsibility for this aspect of company planning, but the strong probability is that the Wilks brothers took the lead. As managing director, S. B. Wilks was used to setting the direction that Rover should take, and he could not have done so at this stage without consulting his brother who, as chief engineer, knew what the company had been working on before the war and what was likely to be feasible.

It was inevitable that both men should have considered the company's previous experience in similar circumstances, and should have looked at what happened immediately after the end of World War I. The period immediately after 1919 had seen a strong demand for small and inexpensive cars, and there was every reason to imagine that the same would happen again. The British economy was likely to remain in the doldrums for at least a few years, which argued against Rover relying on the sort of expensive, high-quality cars that they had been building for the professional classes in the late 1930s.

Rover's first thoughts for a new model turned to an economy-focused small car, the M Model, of which a handful of prototypes were built in 1946.

Similarly, there would be many returning servicemen who wanted to start a new life and would see car ownership as part of that, but who would initially only be able to afford a second-hand one or an inexpensive new one.

It was quite clear to Rover management that the company would be wise to enter the post-war market with a small economy car, perhaps alongside a more traditional Rover or perhaps instead of it for a time. So early thoughts in 1944 were focused on the design of such a machine, and between then and the middle of 1946 the Rover designers and engineers put a great deal of effort into what became known as the M Model. This was a small car, intended for the cheapest 6hp class and essentially a two-seater (although space for children in the rear was also found as the design progressed). The M Model was eventually cancelled before entering production but, as Chapter 3 makes clear, the need to design it brought out considerable inventiveness and ingenuity in the Rover team.

Of course, the M Model was not and could not have been ready for production by the time peace came in May 1945. Although the war still rumbled on in the Far East, it was clear that Europe could begin to return to normality – although it would be a new version of that normality – and that the government would once again permit car production as the need to produce war matériel receded. Rover did not have a new car ready to enter production, and so it did the same as other makers were obliged to do: it made plans to put the cars that it had been building in 1940 back into production until such time as it had something newer to offer.

That was very much easier said than done. At least Rover was fortunate that the jigs and tools associated with the 1940 models had survived the bombing of the Helen Street factory. They were, however, located in Coventry, and Rover planned to restart production at the Solihull factory to which it would relocate entirely during 1945. So, over a period of eight months between March and November that year, the Rover works engineers transported the production tooling and the assembly lines from Coventry to Solihull, where they set it all up and made it ready for use again.

Rover also looked back at the plans for new models it had been working on when car production was halted by the war during 1940. Plans for the 1941-season and later cars had been

Rover's post-war home at Solihull was a factory that had been built to produce aero engine components during World War II.

After the hiatus of the war, Rover re-started manufacture of their pre-war cars. These six-light Saloon models were photographed in front of the main building at Solihull, which still bears traces of wartime camouflage paint. They had been built on the assembly lines that lay behind the administrative offices at the front of the building.

quite well advanced, and the new Rovers were intended to have a sturdy new box-section chassis frame, plus new and highly efficient engines with an inlet-over-exhaust valve arrangement and a sloping cylinder head face. Some ideas for new body designs had also been worked up to the full-size mock-up stage. None of this was lost; all of it could be gathered together and would feed into the thinking about the new full-size post-war Rover saloons. But it could not happen yet. The market had to recover, and Rover had to recover. Nevertheless, as Chapter 4 explains, there is clear evidence that the company began work on those new cars as early as November 1945. They knew them in the beginning as Model P.

Diversification

In addition to work on the Model M and Model P cars, there was a third strand to Rover product development as 1945 came to an end. Between 1940 and 1943, several of the company's senior engineers had been seconded to the jet engine project led by Frank Whittle, and had come to understand these engines very well. Among them had been Maurice Wilks, who had led a team that had redesigned the Whittle engine for greater efficiency, and it had been a development of the Rover-designed engine that had eventually entered production to give Britain its first jet engine. By then, the jet engine work had been handed over to Rolls-Royce, at least partly to prevent strife between Whittle and the Rover people slowing progress on a project seen as vital to Britain's war effort. But Maurice Wilks had not forgotten the experience, and by late 1945 he had gained agreement within Rover that the company should investigate the use of a jet engine – re-named the gas turbine in this instance – to power a road car. This enthusiasm for investigating new avenues of engineering was absolutely typical of the man, and would come to characterise the whole of Rover for many years.

The year 1946 was a critical one for Rover. The company was settling into its new home at Solihull, and on 2 February Sir Stafford Cripps, the President of the Board of Trade, visited the factory to open it officially. Progress on Model M and Model P was slow, and although the first prototypes of Model M would be running by the late summer, the body design for Model P had encountered a number of setbacks. Materials shortages were causing major problems for manufacturing industry, and were behind S. B. Wilks' decision not to introduce the new engines as an interim measure to add appeal to the existing Rover saloon range for 1947.

Developments in the US motor industry also had their effect on Rover's plans, and none more so than the introduction in summer 1946 of the 1947-model Studebakers. Maurice Wilks and production chief Olaf Poppe were already keeping an eye on developments in the USA, and during 1946 they obtained first a Buick and then an Oldsmobile of unspecified type to examine. The US dimension was important, because the American motor industry was some way ahead of its European counterpart at this stage. US car production had not been suspended until 1942, which had allowed two whole years of advance to be made. The US car industry was also able to get back into production with new designs far more quickly than the European industry, and seized the opportunity for yet further advances.

These advances were not only in engineering but also in styling – and in summer 1946 the Studebaker marque stole a march on its rivals by introducing a new approach. Instead of the traditional two-box design that consisted of bonnet and passenger cabin, it announced its 1947 models with a three-box design, where the projecting bonnet was visually balanced by a projecting boot. Though this new approach was controversial, it was an unmistakeable pointer to a new future. It must also have made clear to Maurice Wilks that all the body designs for the new Rover that he had come up with so far had become old-fashioned overnight.

It must also have been very obvious that creating an acceptable modern body style for the planned new Rover was going to take time. Other British manufacturers were already working on new models and Rover could not afford to delay in putting something new on the market. So a plan came together for a stopgap product – an interim saloon that would get something new into the showrooms to retain customer interest while the all-new Rover was being prepared. Rover already had those pre-war designs for a new chassis and a new engine, and by making minimal but valuable alterations to the body design already in production would be able to get a new car ready by early 1948. They gave it the name of P3: Model P had been the original plan for a new saloon, the revived pre-war cars now became P2, and the new car would become the third post-war Rover.

All of these plans were made against a background of increasing difficulty for the motor industry. When Sir Stafford Cripps had formally opened the Solihull factory in February 1946, his speech to the workforce had impressed upon them the need to build for export. Exports would earn revenue that would help rebuild the British economy that had been so hard hit by the cost of the war. By July, the Board of Trade was talking about allocating raw materials – in particular, sheet steel and timber – to manufacturers in accordance with their export performance. A poor export performance would inevitably lead to a lower supply of raw materials, which in turn would restrict the number of cars a manufacturer could produce. In June 1947, S. B. Wilks attended a meeting with government officials in London where those present were told that companies would be expected to export 50 per cent of their output. Later, that figure would be ratcheted up even higher.

Rover's policy of staying with a body style that looked so much like its predecessor now began to look risky. The existing production cars were already looking old-fashioned against newer designs that were becoming available in the export markets where they were sold, and that position was only likely to worsen. If insufficient exports would lead to a reduced supply of raw materials, Rover was going to be in trouble. It was also becoming clear that buyers both at home and overseas did not really want economy cars like the M Model that Rover was preparing; they wanted larger, more exuberant cars to express their freedom in the new post-war world. As 1946 merged into 1947, it was clear that Rover was ill-prepared for the future. If the company was to survive, it needed a new model with guaranteed export appeal that would keep sales alive until the all-new post-war saloon could be introduced.

The solution was not one that anyone could have foreseen. As Chapter 7 explains, Maurice Wilks had obtained a war-surplus military Jeep to help with domestic tasks and for his own amusement. He was struck by how useful it was, and from there to the realisation that there would be a good market for a civilianised equivalent was a small step. Better yet, he knew that new and existing Rover components could be used to create such a vehicle, and that it would not be very difficult to design the other essential elements. By the late summer of 1947, Rover's product plan had therefore been turned on its head. The M Model would not after all go into production. The stopgap P3 model would be prepared for 1948 but its all-new replacement (the P4) would be put into production as soon as humanly possible after that. And the new utility runabout, which gained the name of Land-Rover, would also enter production in 1948 to keep Rover's export quotas up to the required levels.

Building Up Production

One of S. B. Wilks' preoccupations in this period was with increasing Rover production. He had seen the opportunities for increased overall output that the large new factory at Solihull offered, and from the start he envisaged the production of the Model M 6hp cars as additional to the output of full-size Rovers. In August 1946, he told the Rover Board that he wanted to plan for 12–15,000 full-size cars a year, with 5,000 6hp types on top of that total. This was ambitious: it set Rover on track for nearly doubling its pre-war output.

It would be a long time before reality caught up with this vision. Wilks' regular reports to the Board show just how difficult it was to get production numbers up in the post-war climate of materials shortages. In January 1946, production was running at about 30 cars a week; by March it was 70 a week but not consistently; and by May, Rover was making 100 cars a week. The totals steadily increased after that – to 120 a week in July, 135 a week in August and 155 a week in October. By May 1947, Wilks was aiming for 200 a week, but the best so far was 184. The figure of 200 a week was achieved by September, but supply difficulties were limiting further increases. Then in October 1947, Wilks told the Board that he hoped the start of Land-Rover production in spring 1948 would add a further 100 units a week to the factory's output. In due course, it would vastly exceed that; by early 1952 Land-Rover production had reached 400 units a week.

The early months of 1948 must have been both busy and pressured at Solihull, as the company scrambled to get first the new P3 saloons into production and then the new Land-Rover. The P3 cars were announced at the Brussels Autosalon in February, and the Land-Rover at the Amsterdam Show at the end of April. Production took a little time to catch up: full production of all the car variants was not achieved until May, and quantity production of Land-Rovers did not begin until June.

The P3 models did not exactly set the Thames on fire. Although British magazines made loyal noises about the continuation of great British traditions, the feedback from the European continent was that the cars were rather old-fashioned. First-year sales of a little over 6,000 cars were only about 75 per cent of the 8,220 examples of the revived pre-war range that Rover had sold during 1947. The Land-Rover, on the other hand, was a much bigger success than the company had ever imagined. Orders simply poured in after the Amsterdam Show, and by the end of the year the chairman was able to tell the Rover Annual General Meeting that:

> *the orders and enquiries we have already received, particularly from overseas, indicate that this vehicle will be something very much more than an additional source of production. It may yet equal – and even exceed – our car output in quantity.*

EXTRA-CURRICULAR ACTIVITIES

Spare-time activity: this is the Djinn single-seater, with Rover engineer Gordon Bashford on the left.

The Mezzolitre was another club racer built as a spare-time activity. Gordon Bashford is second from the right here.

Most famous of all the club racers associated with Rover engineers was the Rover Special, which was based on the chassis of a Rover prototype.

Despite the restrictions of the austerity period in late-1940s Britain, the enthusiasm of Rover's engineers was undimmed. Outside working hours, chassis designer Gordon Bashford was involved in the design and preparation of two single-seat club racers – the 1100cc Djinn and the 500cc Mezzolitre. His colleagues Spen King, George Mackie and Peter Wilks meanwhile created their own Rover Special single-seater from a redundant Rover prototype (see Chapter 5) and campaigned it with some success.

Unhappy with early designs for a new post-war saloon, Rover used their new chassis and engines under a body that continued the pre-war styling. This is a 1949 four-light P3 model.

The product that ensured Rover's future was a most unlikely one – the utility Land-Rover could hardly have been more different from Rover's refined saloons, but it shared some of their engineering and found a ready market all over the world. This was one of many thousands sold in Australia.

Exports were vital to survival, and there was a ready market in the colonies. This was how the P3 was advertised in Australia.

Britain's Most Versatile Vehicle took Rover into an area of the market that they had never explored before – but the company soon caught up. This advertisement appeared in The Field *magazine for May 1953.*

It did both, and this solid success was followed in the autumn of 1949 by the overdue introduction of the Rover P4 models, the modern Rovers that Maurice Wilks had been trying to achieve since the end of the war. Initial production was hindered by the usual materials shortages, and also by the fact that (just as with the Land-Rover), the launch had actually taken place before the car had been fully developed. Yet the new car was well received. Production and sales built up alongside booming demand for Land-Rovers, and this was supplemented by several overseas assembly operations (which are described in Appendix III). By 1951, Rover was certainly firmly planted back on its feet, and appeared to have a rosy future.

These two strands of revenue-earning activity were supported by a third, because Rover was still producing tank engines on behalf of the government at its Acocks Green factory (*see* Appendix V). There was a fourth one waiting in the wings, in the shape of the gas turbine development work, and before long the ever-enthusiastic Maurice Wilks came up with another new idea for a vehicle that Rover could manufacture.

This time, it was a rugged estate-type vehicle aimed at the farmer's wife, a hybrid of car and Land-Rover that he called the Road-Rover (*see* Chapter 9). So, yet another development project was put in place. This meant that from 1951 Rover's efforts were spread across cars, Land-Rovers, tank engines, gas turbines and the Road-Rover. Most of this was in effect funded by the success of the Land-Rover, but it was a lot for one relatively small company to have on at once, especially as the booming success of the

When the real new post-war Rover arrived in late 1949, it was so different from anything that the company had done before that many conservative-minded buyers were quite upset.

An early P4 model became the first gas turbine Rover prototype. Here it is, with the team that built it.

Gas turbine propulsion was new and exciting, and Rover gained valuable publicity by going public with news of their work. The car was awarded the prestigious RAC Dewar Trophy for outstanding British technical achievement in the automotive industry.

British sports cars cracked the American market, but saloons were less successful. Rover piggy-backed on the Rootes Group's export organisation at first, as this advertisement for the P4 placed by a major Californian car agency shows.

Land-Rover was already calling for further expansion of the manufacturing facilities. Trying to do too much became a Rover characteristic that would endure throughout the 1950s and 1960s, and it would only be curbed after the company became part of British Leyland in 1968.

Nevertheless, level-headed management by the Rover Board coped admirably with all this activity. The need for more Land-Rover manufacturing facilities was addressed during 1952 when the company bought new premises at Perry Barr and at Springfield and expanded its London Service Depot at Seagrave Road by buying adjacent premises. (There is more detail about all these sites in Appendix II.) Plans to erect a further 80,000sq ft building at Solihull were also approved, but were deferred because of a worsening financial climate.

In mid-1952, a new share issue brought in the finance needed for an ambitious expansion plan that also incorporated some more new products. The expansion programme for the twelve months between August 1952 and August 1953 embraced the introduction of two new variants of the Rover saloon range (the 60 and the 90), two Land-Rover models (the 86 and the 107) to replace the single existing one, and the Road-Rover. In addition, it would cover the start of gas turbine engine production (initially as auxiliary power plants – *see* Chapter 6). And, as Chapter 9 explains, Maurice Wilks was already focusing on another new range of cars and engines before the end of 1953, as well as on special-bodied derivatives of the existing cars. The seemingly

This early 1950s picture inside the Rover works shows an early Land-Rover and an eclectic group of three competitor vehicles that the company had bought for evaluation. They are a Citroën 2CV, a Porsche 356 and a Panhard Dyna. Just visible on the right is the front wing of a Road-Rover prototype.

Taken probably inside the Rover Service Department, this picture shows several P3 models from the late 1940s and (second from left) a solitary P4.

'To the casual glance two more dissimilar vehicles could not be imagined.' *Cars and Land-Rovers tended to be advertised separately, but there were a few instances where they appeared together. This advertisement was placed in the* Illustrated London News *of June 1953. It is easy now to forget the heritage behind the hugely successful Land-Rover, not least because that marque survives but Rover ceased to exist in 2005.*

unflappable Board once again coped with all of this, and during 1953 decided it would be wise to increase its membership maximum from seven to twelve directors – a proposal that would be discussed at the Annual General Meeting at the end of the year.

All this was happening at Rover against a social and economic background that had still not fully recovered from the war years and the subsequent period of austerity. Clothes were rationed until 1949, and both soap and petrol were rationed until 1950. New private cars had been scarce in Britain thanks to the Government's insistence on giving priority to exports, and although restrictions were easing, some were still in place. A huge increase in purchase tax in the 1951 Budget threatened sales of many of the more expensive cars. Exports were still top of the priorities in 1952, and although the Home Quota for both cars and Land-Rovers was increased in the middle of the year, production totals of the basic Land-Rover for the 1953 season were some 20 per cent down as compared to 1952. Britain was not out of the woods yet – but Rover was thriving and was more than ready to face the challenges of the new decade.

Export requirements introduced some new procedures to Rover. These left-hand-drive models were pictured on the dockside before being loaded aboard the cargo ship that would take them to their destination. They are fitted with 'slave' tyres made of wooden blocks; the real thing would be fitted at the end of their journey.

Journey's end – almost. This group of Land-Rovers has been unloaded at docks in India and will now be transported, in most cases by rail, to the ordering dealers.

From autumn 1953, the wheelbase size of the basic Land-Rover was increased to 86in, and the rear overhang was lengthened to provide greater load space. A new seven-seat Station Wagon, seen here, followed soon after.

Also from autumn 1953, a long-wheelbase companion model on a 107in wheelbase was introduced. It was specifically designed as a load-carrier, with a 6ft long load bed.

At the same time as two new Land-Rover models appeared, so did two new variants of the P4 saloon, the 60 and the 90. This view of a 60 shows two key interior changes – to a side-mounted handbrake and a floor-mounted gearchange. The handbrake later went back to its earlier position.

PRODUCTION FIGURES, 1946–53

These figures are for the Rover 'production year', which did not usually correspond directly with the calendar year. The production year for Rover cars and for Land-Rovers was not always the same, and the figures in the 'Total' column should therefore be treated with caution, although they do give a good idea of the company's health for each year. The car production figures for 1951 were artificially inflated by a long model-year.

1946 The production year corresponded to the calendar year, but the production figure shown includes a handful of cars completed in December 1945.

1947 Production year figures appear to correspond to the calendar year, plus January 1948 (13 months).

1948 The car production year ran from February to December 1948. The Land-Rover production year ran from March 1948 to March 1949.

1949 The car production year ran from January 1949 to July or August 1949. The Land-Rover production year ran from February to July 1949.

1950 The car production year ran from September 1949 to August 1950. The Land-Rover production year ran from July 1949 to March 1950.

1951 The car production year ran from September 1950 to December 1951. The Land-Rover production year ran from September 1950 to August 1951.

1952 The car production year ran from January 1952 to August (September?) 1952. The Land-Rover production year ran from July 1951 to August 1952.

1953 The car production year ran from October 1952 to July 1953. The Land-Rover production year ran from September 1952 to August 1953.

	Cars	*Land-Rovers*	*Total*
1946	5,115		5,115
1947	8,220		8,220
1948	6,123	3,000	9,123
1949	2,989	5,000	7,989
1950	5,250	15,999	21,249
1951	10,976	17,358	28,334
1952	5,750	18,715	24,465
1953	8,000	22,272	30,272

The early 1950s saw the first tentative steps to create a model called the Road-Rover. It never did make production, but was an interesting hybrid of Rover car and Land-Rover thinking. This is believed to be the first prototype.

CHAPTER 2

Back in Business, 1946–47

World War II was drawing slowly to a close by the start of 1945, when the British government issued permits for car manufacture to begin again. At their meeting on 15 January, the members of the Rover Board learned that they had been granted a permit to build 1,100 cars, or just over 10 per cent of their typical annual output by the end of the 1930s. It was not a lot, but the chances of achieving even that small number looked very slim.

As most of the tooling for the 1940-model Rovers had been put into storage for the duration of hostilities, the decision about what to do more or less made itself. There was in any case no other realistic option if Rover wanted to get back into business quickly: even though plans for new models were in their early stages, these would take time to be developed into viable production models. Rover would have to re-start manufacture of the cars that they had been building

The post-war chassis was barely altered from the one that Rover had been building when war broke out in 1939. This chassis of a 1940-model Twelve was typical.

Rover advertising of the period was always discreet, as this rare colour advertisement shows.

when the war brought production to a halt five years earlier. The company was not alone among British manufacturers in being forced to such a conclusion.

On the positive side, it was already clear that by taking over the shadow factory at Solihull that it had been managing for the Ministry of Aircraft Production, Rover could provide for future expansion. The Solihull factory was larger and newer than the old Rover factory at Helen Street in Coventry, and it was well sited for rail and road links (although there would never be a railhead at the factory itself). Rover had already investigated the possibility of buying it outright but the MAP had declined to sell, although they were prepared to consider a long-term lease. So, at its February 1945 meeting, the Rover Board agreed to lease the Solihull factory and to dispose of both the Helen Street works and the small factory at Clay Lane in Coventry. Not mentioned at that meeting, but also important to Rover's plans, was the Tyseley factory that could be converted back to its pre-war function as an engine and gearbox assembly plant.

So it was that in the eight months between March and November 1945, the Rover Works Engineers moved all the necessary tools and machinery from the company's old factory in Coventry to its new one in Solihull, and re-established the company's production and assembly facilities there. In the meantime, Rover prepared a very much slimmed-down range for production, focusing on the models that they believed would have most appeal in the straitened circumstances of a post-war economy.

The Ten Coupé, the Twenty Sports Saloon and the elegant Salmons-bodied six-cylinder Drophead Coupés of the pre-war range were therefore not revived. The new post-war range would consist of six-light Saloons on the four-cylinder Ten and Twelve and the six-cylinder Fourteen and Sixteen chassis, plus four-light Sports Saloons on the Twelve, Fourteen and Sixteen. All these names reflected the RAC horsepower rating that governed the annual tax payable. Visually, the cars were to be unchanged from their 1940 predecessors. Saloons would have a horn mounted on the left-hand dumb-iron and a pass lamp to match it on the right, while Sports Saloons would retain their centrally mounted pass lamp and twin horns. However, Rover did find time to make a few improvements as well. They changed the double-helical gears in the gearbox to single-helical types and modified the shaft bearing arrangement to suit. On the two six-cylinder chassis, Armstrong dampers with vertical pistons replaced the earlier Luvax type.

Prices for these first post-war cars had been agreed by late November 1945, and were inevitably much higher than they had been in 1940: a Ten Saloon that had been £275 now cost £460 even before the new purchase tax was added, and a Sixteen Sports Saloon – which would not be available for some months – last priced at £370 all-in was now £595 before the new tax, which put its price up to £761 0s 7d. These were simply enormous increases.

According to George Oliver (in *The Rover*), a pilot-production line was set up at the Clay Lane factory at the end of the year, while the Solihull factory was still being prepared for its new role. Here, about 30 staff assembled the first post-war Rovers – all of them four-cylinder Saloons. Oliver notes that a photograph of two Ten Saloons about to leave the Solihull factory appeared in the press towards the end of 1945, and no doubt this was issued to commemorate the start of production. The despatch records confirm that production had actually begun in November, and that the Ten models had been followed before the end of the month by the first Twelves and in December by the first Sixteens. By the end of the year probably around 35 cars had been completed altogether.

The Tens may have been the first to be built, but back in July 1945 the first post-war Rover sales brochure listed only the Sixteen, which was promised with either the six-light Saloon or four-light Sports Saloon body, in either case with a sliding roof. However, by October the plan to re-introduce four chassis types was in place, and

The pre-war OHV engines were also put back into production in 1945. This is a four-cylinder type...

...and this is a six-cylinder type. Though not up to more modern standards, these engines were still highly respected.

This sales brochure was dated July 1945 and was for export markets. It was entirely focused on the Sixteen models, of which production would not begin until December – and the four-light Sports Saloon would not follow until mid-1946. The cover design was again discreet, but the embossed cardboard gave it a quality feel that was consistent with the Rover image.

A 1946-model Rover body going through the spray booth at the new works in Solihull. It would have been painted black.

One of the most interesting stages of car assembly was always that where body met chassis. Here it is on the Rover assembly line in 1946.

These 1946 models were pictured on the finishing line, where they were being inspected for imperfections under bright lighting. They had already been road-tested.

The Motor of 3 October carried a four-page article entitled 'Announcing the Post-war Range of Rover Cars', which explained what was to happen.

A few early production cars were sent to the Rover experimental department, which was then still located at the old Helen Street works in Coventry. Several more went to senior members of the Rover staff, who were no doubt asked to evaluate them carefully. A small number went to the London distributor Henlys during December, and others were shipped before the end of the month to other major distributors, but the numbers at this stage were tiny.

All these first post-war Rovers were six-light Saloons, and all of them were finished in black with gold fine lines and brown leather upholstery. The Tens, Twelves and Sixteens were joined in production during January 1946 by Fourteen Saloons after a single example had been completed in December, and that month S. B. Wilks told the Rover Board that the assembly lines were turning out about six cars a day, which meant about 30 cars a week. This was achieved in the face of raw materials shortages and other supply difficulties, and the Rover Board minutes from this period regularly refer to such problems. Some cars were built with cloth upholstery to keep the lines moving when there were shortages of leather, and cloth is actually listed in the parts catalogue for the early post-war cars. A shortage of materials for chrome plating resulted in some early Tens leaving the factory with black-painted radiator shells and black-painted sidelight bodies, and a change from SU to Solex carburettors for the four-cylinder engines a few months after production began was almost certainly another result of supply difficulties.

All these hindrances to production persuaded Rover to play it safe for the first half of 1946 by restricting the number of variations in production: four models with just one combination of paint and upholstery were quite enough to cope with for the time being. Production quantities did increase, but it was a gradual process. By March Rover were building 70 cars a week, and by July that figure had increased to 120, although there were still supply difficulties and the prices of materials were increasing as well. It was also in July that S. B. Wilks recommended to his colleagues on the Board that Rover should raise showroom prices to cover these increases.

Exports had begun in late January, the first being a Ten Saloon that was one of several shipped to Skandinavsk Motors in Denmark. Sales catalogues nevertheless strongly suggest that Rover pinned their export hopes very much on the Sixteen. Some overseas countries also took Twelves, but it appears that the Fourteens were not generally available for export. Other overseas destinations were Belgium (Etablissements Paul Sterckx), Malta (St Joseph Garage) and South Africa (Robb Motors in Capetown), and all the cars for these countries appear to have had right-hand drive. For the moment, Rover was able to get away with not having left-hand-drive cars to offer, because such was the hunger for new cars in many of its export territories that buyers were prepared to settle for a car with its steering wheel on the 'wrong' side rather than no car at all.

Nevertheless, there was never any doubt that this would be a short-lived phenomenon; most European countries were going to need cars with their steering wheel on the left, and this therefore became a development priority. In addition,

This 1946 Ten was typical of the P2 Rovers but would have been black when it left the factory; no alternative colours were available in the beginning.

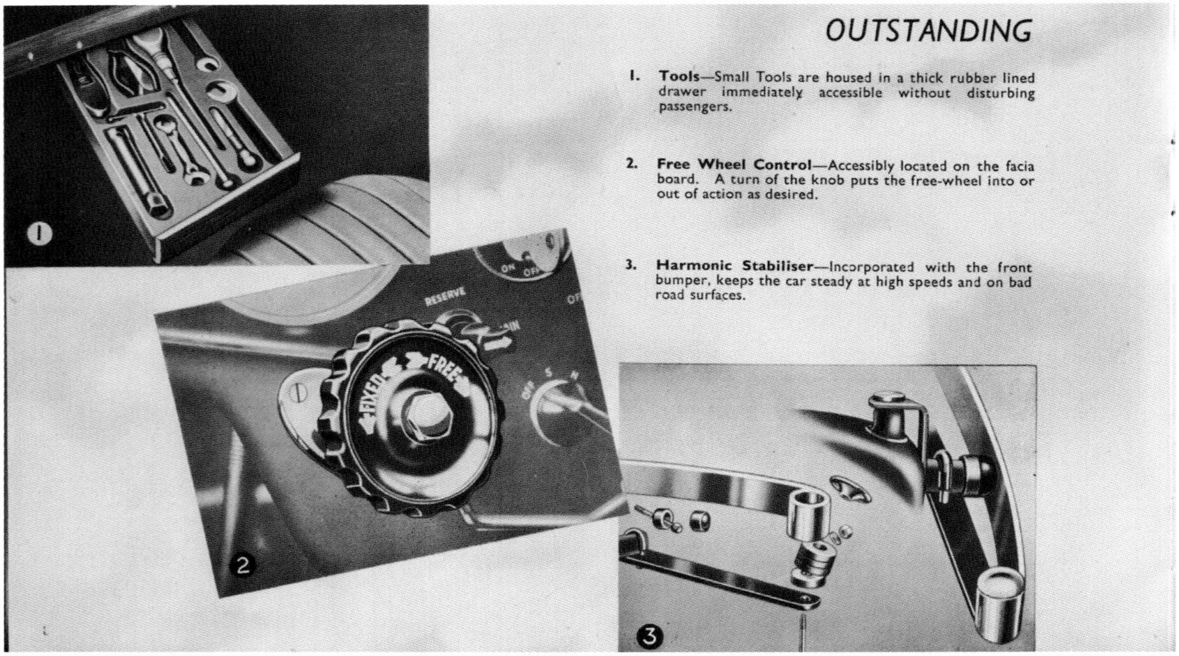

OUTSTANDING

1. **Tools**—Small Tools are housed in a thick rubber lined drawer immediately accessible without disturbing passengers.

2. **Free Wheel Control**—Accessibly located on the facia board. A turn of the knob puts the free-wheel into or out of action as desired.

3. **Harmonic Stabiliser**—Incorporated with the front bumper, keeps the car steady at high speeds and on bad road surfaces.

The sepia tint of the July 1945 sales brochure's inside pages was perfectly in keeping with the discreet Rover image. It may also have been necessary, as colour printing was considered a luxury in the austerity years after the war. This left-hand page displays some of the features that Rover described as 'outstanding'…

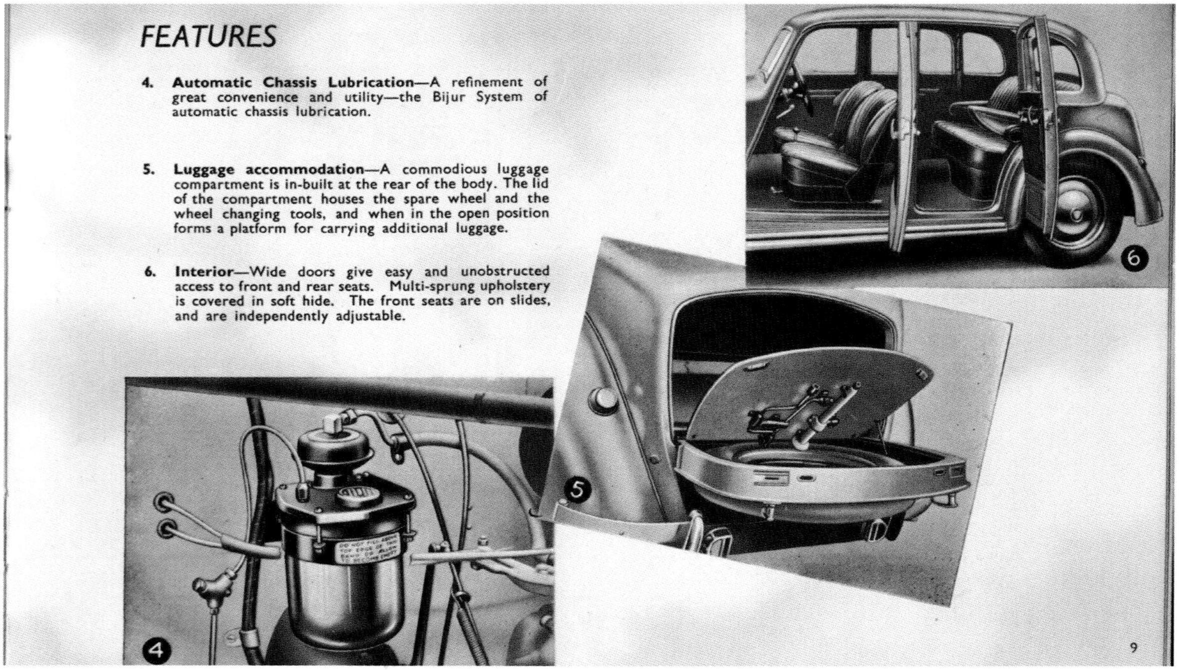

FEATURES

4. **Automatic Chassis Lubrication**—A refinement of great convenience and utility—the Bijur System of automatic chassis lubrication.

5. **Luggage accommodation**—A commodious luggage compartment is in-built at the rear of the body. The lid of the compartment houses the spare wheel and the wheel changing tools, and when in the open position forms a platform for carrying additional luggage.

6. **Interior**—Wide doors give easy and unobstructed access to front and rear seats. Multi-sprung upholstery is covered in soft hide. The front seats are on slides, and are independently adjustable.

9

… and this right-hand page described a few more. The pictures almost certainly showed pre-war models – but there was no difference in features like these.

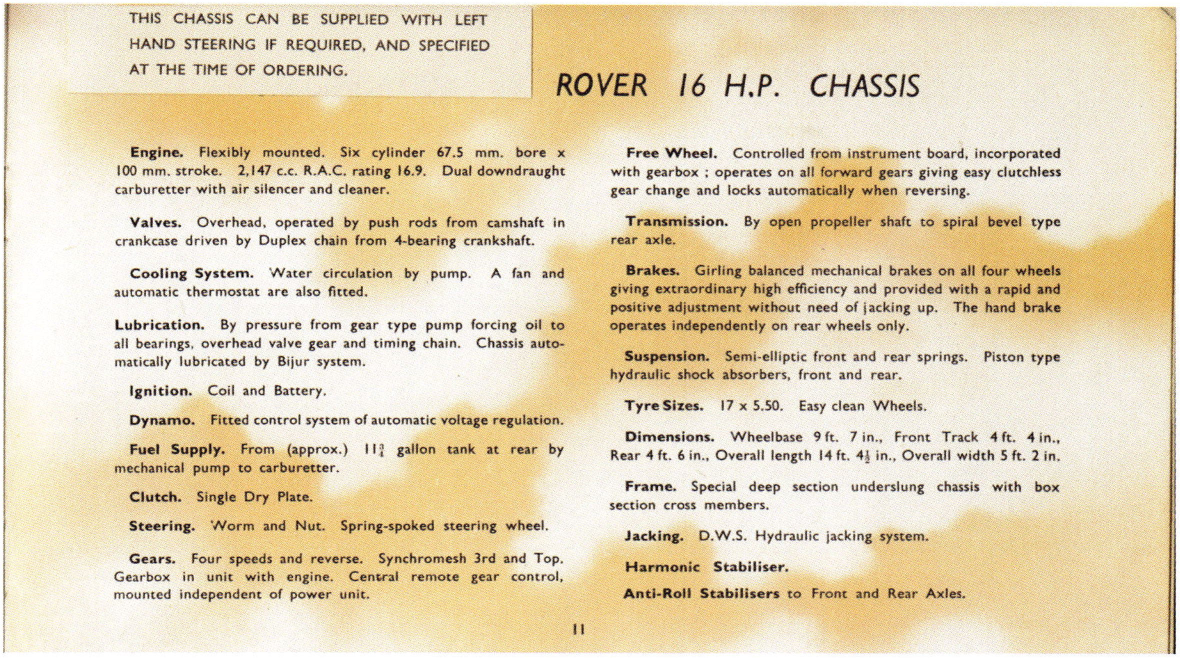

THIS CHASSIS CAN BE SUPPLIED WITH LEFT HAND STEERING IF REQUIRED, AND SPECIFIED AT THE TIME OF ORDERING.

ROVER 16 H.P. CHASSIS

Engine. Flexibly mounted. Six cylinder 67.5 mm. bore x 100 mm. stroke. 2,147 c.c. R.A.C. rating 16.9. Dual downdraught carburetter with air silencer and cleaner.

Valves. Overhead, operated by push rods from camshaft in crankcase driven by Duplex chain from 4-bearing crankshaft.

Cooling System. Water circulation by pump. A fan and automatic thermostat are also fitted.

Lubrication. By pressure from gear type pump forcing oil to all bearings, overhead valve gear and timing chain. Chassis automatically lubricated by Bijur system.

Ignition. Coil and Battery.

Dynamo. Fitted control system of automatic voltage regulation.

Fuel Supply. From (approx.) 11¾ gallon tank at rear by mechanical pump to carburetter.

Clutch. Single Dry Plate.

Steering. Worm and Nut. Spring-spoked steering wheel.

Gears. Four speeds and reverse. Synchromesh 3rd and Top. Gearbox in unit with engine. Central remote gear control, mounted independent of power unit.

Free Wheel. Controlled from instrument board, incorporated with gearbox ; operates on all forward gears giving easy clutchless gear change and locks automatically when reversing.

Transmission. By open propeller shaft to spiral bevel type rear axle.

Brakes. Girling balanced mechanical brakes on all four wheels giving extraordinary high efficiency and provided with a rapid and positive adjustment without need of jacking up. The hand brake operates independently on rear wheels only.

Suspension. Semi-elliptic front and rear springs. Piston type hydraulic shock absorbers, front and rear.

Tyre Sizes. 17 x 5.50. Easy clean Wheels.

Dimensions. Wheelbase 9 ft. 7 in., Front Track 4 ft. 4 in., Rear 4 ft. 6 in., Overall length 14 ft. 4½ in., Overall width 5 ft. 2 in.

Frame. Special deep section underslung chassis with box section cross members.

Jacking. D.W.S. Hydraulic jacking system.

Harmonic Stabiliser.

Anti-Roll Stabilisers to Front and Rear Axles.

11

The sticker promising availability of models with left-hand drive was clearly an afterthought – and despite this July 1945 promise, there would be no left-hand-drive cars until around a year later.

some countries required speedometers marked in kilometres per hour rather than miles per hour. Fortunately, the symmetrical design of the existing Rover dashboard, with its instruments in the centre, did not cause any major difficulties in creating left-hand-drive models.

Behind the scenes, Rover was dealing with a multitude of problems. Preparing the Solihull factory for its new role was only one of them. Equally difficult was finding the staff to operate it; many skilled men had been away fighting during the war, and it would be some time before they returned to the UK and were ready for work again. There was also the complication of new government employment regulations; though designed to prevent abuses, they certainly made it harder for manufacturing industries to take on the staff they needed.

Then there were more new government regulations. Sir Stafford Cripps had given a hint of what was to come when he had formally opened the Solihull factory. He had 'encouraged' the Rover workforce to help rebuild the British economy by producing cars for export. For the next few years, there would be considerable pressure on British manufacturing industry of all kinds to prioritise exports over catering for the Home market. As chairman E. Ransom Harrison said in his statement to the Rover AGM in December 1946, 'in support of the government's policy, we immediately formed an export department, and we are taking every possible step to develop this side of our business'. But this new focus on exports must have seemed very strange to a company that had never taken overseas sales very seriously before.

Mid-Season Changes

It is not clear from surviving records when the first left-hand-drive Rovers were actually built, but it was probably in summer 1946. A few months earlier, Rover had amended their chassis numbering system, adding an R prefix

At the top end of the range, this was a Sixteen six-cylinder Saloon. It is a 1947 model, in the maroon that became available from summer 1946.

Grey suited the cars very well, and is seen here on a left-hand-drive Sixteen dating from 1947.

The Cheshire police force was a regular user of Rovers in the late 1940s and early 1950s, and bought this four-cylinder saloon, probably a Twelve, in early 1947. The auxiliary light has been fitted on a special pedestal.

to cars built for export with right-hand drive; in due course, an L prefix would be added to those with left-hand drive. Home market cars had no additional prefix. This new system was perhaps a convincing way of recording how much effort the company was putting into building vehicles for export, and quoting the full chassis number would also alert its parts department to any peculiarities associated with export specifications. However, things were never quite that simple: production shortages, cancelled orders, export shipping difficulties and a host of other problems intervened from time to time to ensure that some export right-hand-drive cars were sold on the home market while some home market cars went for export.

Two more important changes that took place in summer 1946 reflected Rover's growing confidence. In late June, the six-light Saloons were supplemented by four-light Sports Saloon derivatives of the Twelve and Fourteen, and the first Sixteen Sports Saloons were made in July. Meanwhile, in what must have seemed like a fit of exuberance at the time, the first few alternatives to black with brown upholstery also appeared when blue, green and maroon cars with matching upholstery colours all became available.

Despite this apparent new confidence, production was still having its ups and downs. Just 5,115 cars left the Solihull factory between the end of 1945 and the end of 1946, which was less than half of Rover's 1939 total.

The 1947 Models

Production of the 1947 models began in January that year, after a single Ten Saloon had served as a pilot model at the end of December 1946. The new cars were released to the public on

The four-light design and blind rear quarters of the Sports Saloon models certainly gave them a more sporting appearance, but they were still very obviously pre-war in design.

14 January, and incorporated several valuable changes of specification. A Clayton-Dewandre heater-demister was now standard, and a red temperature-controlled choke warning light replaced the trafficator telltale on the dashboard. The driver's seat on Saloon models could now be adjusted for height. A change to the Luvax system added direct feeds to each front axle swivel pin in place of the earlier single supply to the centre of the axle beam, and the Twelves now took on vertical-piston Armstrong dampers like the two six-cylinder cars. At the same time, the centre of the facia was reshaped with a flat lower edge that allowed the installation of a new optional car radio. Though expensive, the Radiomobile 100 that Rover recommended was very much state-of-the-art and became a prized possession in the late 1940s.

If all had gone according to plan, the 1947-model Sports Saloons would have become the first Rovers to enter production with the new inlet-over-exhaust engines under their bonnets. That certainly had been S. B. Wilks' intention, but at the September 1946 meeting of the Rover Board he told his fellow directors that he had decided not to go ahead with it – mainly, it appears, because of continuing serious shortages of coal as well as steel. As a result, the new engines would be held over for a year, until the new Rover P3 saloons that were then under development were introduced. Meanwhile, those shortages may have been the reason for a minor specification change during 1947. The Sixteen had been introduced with two ventilator flaps on each side of its bonnet, while the Ten, Twelve and Fourteen all had plain bonnet sides. Yet it appears that 250 Sixteen Saloons and 50 Sixteen Sports Saloons were built with Fourteen-pattern bonnets that had plain sides.

Exports remained vital to the country's well-being, and to Rover's. For 1947 there would be more left-hand-drive types – Sixteen Sports

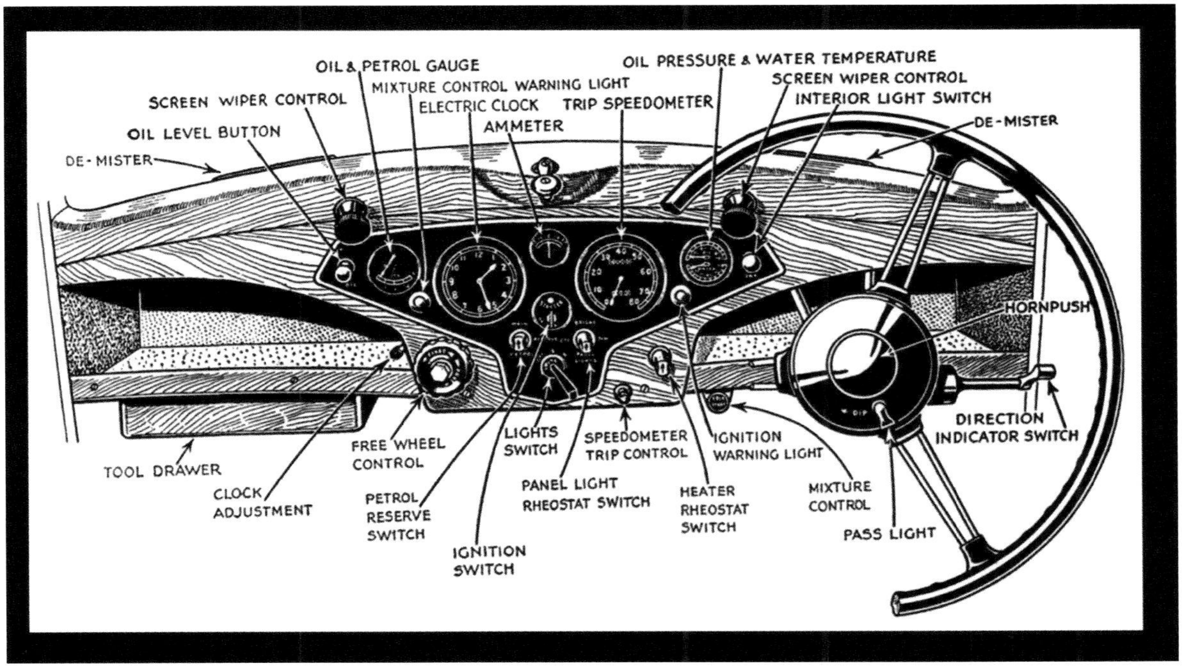

The pre-war dashboard was modified with a straight bottom edge so that a radio set could be fitted. This was, of course, an extra-cost option.

The tool drawer under the dashboard contained a selection of hand tools to enable an owner to carry out basic adjustment and maintenance. This one is from a 1946 car.

Saloons and Ten Saloons. All cars for export would have SU electric fuel pumps, as used on some 1946 export models, instead of the AC mechanical pumps that were otherwise standard. Some export cars would also get special cooling arrangements consisting of a cowl behind the radiator and a four-bladed aluminium fan like that fitted to the 20hp models before the war.

Production dropped slightly as Rover made the change to the 1947 specification on the assembly lines, and in January S. B. Wilks reported that production was running at 140 cars a week. But full recovery was still a long way off, and the position deteriorated almost immediately. Countrywide power cuts accompanied a very severe winter, and Rover production was forced to stop on 7 February. After a two-week shutdown, power was restored to the midlands on Monday 24 February, but allocations of solid fuel were considerably reduced. S. B. Wilks wanted to aim for an output of 120 cars a week, but in March the Rover Board agreed to settle for 100 cars a week, which was just enough to allow the company to break even. That same month, major increases in the showroom prices of all Rover models bore their own witness to the problems of the period.

Yet Rover were clearly determined to press on with new features that would make their cars as attractive as possible. The Sixteen Sports Saloons became available with two-colour paint schemes from summer 1947 after a first example went for export in March. There were both discreet ones (such as black with maroon or green with grey) and flamboyant ones (Sundown Fawn with brown), but the two-colour schemes seem not to have been mentioned in sales literature and it is not clear whether they cost extra. One way or another, Rover clearly decided that they were to be confined to the top of the range models only. The single two-colour Twelve Sports Saloon built in August 1947 was probably a trial of some kind, and remained unique.

The 1947 Tourers

By the end of 1946 if not earlier, Rover knew that it needed a model with greater appeal in overseas markets, and that it needed one as quickly as possible. There could be no question of developing anything entirely new – development resources were fully committed to future new saloon models – and so the company chose to draw up a new Tourer body for the existing Twelve chassis. To avoid disrupting assembly lines that were already under strain, the decision was taken to sub-contract the assembly of the special bodies to another company.

The Twelve Tourer was certainly intended to boost Rover exports, which were barely meeting government targets. Maurice Wilks must have taken the lead in designing the body, with Ben Loker preparing the drawings. Len Jackman, who was Rover's works manager, became

The 1947 Twelve Tourer was intended primarily for export, but most were actually sold on the home market. It was a clear warning to Rover that their cars did not yet have the necessary appeal to sell well overseas.

The Twelve Tourer was a well-resolved design, but lacked the lightness of its pre-war counterpart. This one was pictured in June 1947.

involved as well, and when he retired at the end of April he was retained in an advisory capacity, 'particularly in connection with the manufacture of Tourer and Special bodies', according to the minutes of the Rover Board meeting on 26 March that year.

The design of the new body was not entirely straightforward, despite its similarities to the Tourers that Rover had built between 1934 and 1936. The jigs for these had long gone, and even the drawings had been lost when the old Rover factory in Coventry was bombed during

PRICES FOR ROVER MODELS, 1946–47

A surviving letter from Rover dealer Albert Farnell of Bradford makes clear that Rover had informed its dealers of the initial prices by late November 1945.

Note that the Twelve Tourer was never listed in Rover catalogues and that its price remains unknown.

January 1946			
	Retail price	***Purchase tax***	***Total cost***
Ten Saloon	£460	£128 10s 7d	£588 10s 7d
Twelve Saloon	£505	£141 0s 7d	£646 0s 7d
Twelve Sports Saloon	£520	£145 3s 11d	£665 3s 11d
Fourteen Saloon	£550	£153 10s 7d	£703 10s 7d
Fourteen Sports Saloon	£565	£157 13s 11d	£722 13s 11d
Sixteen Saloon	£580	£161 17s 3d	£741 17s 3d
Sixteen Sports Saloon	£595	£166 0s 7d	£761 0s 7d

January 1947			
	Retail price	***Purchase tax***	***Total cost***
Ten Saloon	£575	£160 9s 6d	£735 9s 6d
Twelve Saloon	£615	£171 11s 8d	£786 11s 8d
Twelve Sports Saloon	£630	£175 15s 10d	£805 15s 10d
Fourteen Saloon	£655	£182 13s 11d	£837 13s 11d
Fourteen Sports Saloon	£670	£186 17s 3d	£856 17s 3d
Sixteen Saloon	£670	£186 17s 3d	£856 17s 3d
Sixteen Sports Saloon	£685	£191 0s 7d	£876 0s 7d

March 1947			
	Retail price	***Purchase tax***	***Total cost***
Ten Saloon	£632 10s 0d	£176 8s 11d	£808 18s 11d
Twelve Saloon	£676 10s 0d	£188 13s 4d	£865 3s 4d
Twelve Sports Saloon	£693 0s 0d	£193 5s 0d	£886 5s 0d
Fourteen Saloon	£720 10s 0d	£200 17s 10d	£921 7s 10d
Fourteen Sports Saloon	£737 0s 0d	£205 9s 6d	£942 9s 6d
Sixteen Saloon	£737 0s 0d	£205 9s 6d	£942 9s 6d
Sixteen Sports Saloon	£753 10s 0d	£210 1s 2d	£963 11s 2d

the war. The company therefore decided to buy back one of its own pre-war Tourers and use it as a template for their new design. The car they found was a 1935 model on the Twelve chassis, which had been registered as JN 4364.

There would be many differences between the pre-war and post-war Tourers, though. For a start, the smaller 17-inch wheels and helmet-type wings of the post-war Rovers greatly altered the proportions of the earlier design. Rover also chose to align the new Tourers visually with their other post-war models by fitting the twin horns and central pass lamp from the then-current Sports Saloons. A comprehensive redesign of the rear saw the spare wheel mounted inside the boot, as it was on the latest Rover saloons. Although the overall result was neat and attractive, the more voluminous wings, redesigned tail and steel disc wheels made the cars look heavier and much less sporting than their pre-war counterparts. On the first seventeen cars, there was a folding windscreen, but this was then changed for a fixed one.

By May 1947, Rover had agreed to sub-contract body manufacture to AP Aircraft Ltd, who rented a portion of Rover's own Clay Lane factory for the purpose. The initials 'AP' stood for Austin and Perks, the two owners of AP Aircraft Ltd, which was a small company that had started out as a supplier to the midlands aircraft industry during the years leading up to the war. They also assembled car bodies for other manufacturers, including Lea Francis, on the Clay Lane site. In the style of independent coachbuilders, they put their own small brass manufacturer's plate on the Tourer bodies, reading, 'Coachwork by APA Ltd, Stoke Row, Coventry'. The contract with Rover probably called for a specified number of these cars to be built, and in practice 200 were completed before the end of 1947.

Some commentators have suggested that Rover actually built the first few bodies, but it seems more likely that they were constructed at Clay Lane. There was nevertheless a change in design after the first four or five had been made, when the rather angular lines of the tail were rounded off slightly. This may have simplified manufacture as much as it improved the appearance. Rover gave the Tourers their own chassis number sequence, and actually produced special versions of the Twelve chassis for them, with four triangular strengthening plates welded to the cross-member just behind the gearbox, and rear springs from the 10hp to suit their lighter bodywork.

The same 'outstanding features' photographs were used again here – but this 1946 sales catalogue for the Sixteen was printed in Spanish and was for Uruguay.

Even though the 1947 Twelve Tourer was an export model, every one of the 200 made had right-hand drive, which inevitably limited the number of countries where it could be sold. Surviving records show that only 150 of these had chassis numbers with the R prefix that indicated an export model, so the other 50 must always have been intended for sale on the home market. The proportions were carefully judged: the 150 cars for export were 75 per cent of the 200 total, and thus exceeded the government requirement for export production. Unfortunately, export production and export sales were not at all the same thing.

In practice, export sales of the Tourer were disappointing. Of the 150 cars earmarked for export, 110 were actually sold in Britain in addition to the 50 cars intended for home market sale. Of the 40 cars actually exported, which represented a miserable 20 per cent of the total, the largest number (nineteen cars) went to India. Ten went to Dewar's Garage in Calcutta, six to Rane in Madras, and the remaining three to Garware in Bombay, where they were no doubt mainly bought by British expats. There were six cars each for Ceylon and South Africa, two each for Venezuela and Uruguay, and Cyprus, Malta, Sweden, Thailand and Trinidad all had one each.

Unexplained is that none of the Tourers went to Australia, which was generally receptive to Rovers. Nevertheless, the message from the Tourer experiment was clear: Rover still badly needed a model that would appeal to overseas buyers.

The End of the Line

Materials supply shortages continued during 1947 and, in May, Rover had to cut back temporarily to a four-day working week because of them. The

CHASSIS NUMBERS AND PRODUCTION TOTALS, 1946–47 P2 ROVERS

The chassis number sequences and production totals for the 1946–47 period are taken from the records of the despatch department at Solihull. All new cars passed to this department from the production lines, and were then 'despatched' against orders to dealers, distributors, or private individuals. The despatch records were kept in hand-written ledgers, which are now preserved in the archives of the British Motor Museum at Gaydon.

Note that a dash is used here between the identifying type prefix and the serial number to aid clarity; it does not appear on the chassis plates themselves.

Season	*Type*	*Body type*	*Chassis sequence*	*Total*
1946	Ten	Saloon	611-0001 – 611-1340	1,340
	Twelve	Saloon	621-0001 – 621-1580	1,580
		Sports Saloon	623-0001 – 623-0240	240
	Fourteen	Saloon	631-0001 – 631-0620	620
		Sports Saloon	633-0001 – 633-0235	235
	Sixteen	Saloon	641-0001 – 641-0875	875
		Sports Saloon	643-0001 – 643-0225	225
1947	Ten	Saloon	711-0001 – 711-1300	1,300
	Twelve	Saloon	721-0001 – 721-2300	2,300
		Sports Saloon	723-0001 – 723-0520	520
		Tourer	725-0001 – 725-0200	200
	Fourteen	Saloon	731-0001 – 731-0700	700
		Sports Saloon	733-0001 – 733-0150	150
	Sixteen	Saloon	741-0001 – 741-2325	2,325
		Sports Saloon	743-0001 – 743-0725	725

position did improve slowly, but supply difficulties were still limiting output in September, when the Rover Board heard the good news that car production in recent weeks had actually exceeded its target of 200 units. The position continued to improve, though slowly, and by the end of the year Rover could claim a build total of 8,220 cars. It was still not up to pre-war standards, but it showed promise.

The government was still pushing for exports above home market deliveries, and planned in future to set a ceiling on allocations of raw materials for home market cars; it also wanted greater standardisation of designs to streamline production. By October 1947, the requirement was that 75 per cent of all production must be exported. It was fortunate that by that stage Rover had come up with a new idea for a product that would appeal in overseas markets, as Chapter 7 shows.

The last of the revived pre-war models were built in January 1948, and then Solihull went flat-out to prepare the manufacturing facilities and the assembly lines for the new P3 models.

COLOURS AND TRIMS, 1946–47 P2 ROVERS

The same colours and combinations were used in both the 1946 and the 1947 seasons.

The only two-tone colour schemes offered as standard were for the 1947 Sixteen Sports Saloons. Wheels were painted to match the bodywork. All radiator stoneguards were enamelled in silver and all woodwork was polished walnut.

Leather upholstery was standard, but some cars from both years of production had cloth for both the seat facings and the main door panels, and the parts catalogue lists cloth in the same four colours as the leather.

Body colour	Fine lines	Upholstery
Black	Gold	Brown
Black	Green	Green
Dark Blue	Grey	Blue
Green	Green	Green
Grey	Blue	Blue
Maroon	Gold	Maroon

The two-tone paint schemes available from summer 1947 for the Sixteen Sports Saloons were as follows. (The figures have been calculated from the despatch department records.)

Black and Maroon	from March 1947; 50 recorded
Black and Blue	from June 1947; 2 recorded
Grey and Maroon	from June 1947; 34 recorded
Sundown Fawn and Brown	from October 1947; 20 recorded
Grey and Green	from October 1947; 18 recorded
Grey and Blue	from December 1947; one recorded
Green and Green	from December 1947; one recorded (possibly a mis-recording of Grey and Green)

CHAPTER 3

Inspiration: Small Wonder

Like every other British car manufacturer during the 1939–1945 conflict, Rover were expected to devote all their resources to the war effort. There was no chance that they would be able to re-start car production until peace returned, and so there was no point in putting any effort into designing any new models. At least, that was the theory; in practice, post-war car production was probably never very far from the thoughts of those who served on the Rover Board, although there is no evidence of what they were thinking in the minutes that record that Board's meetings.

No doubt it was S. B. Wilks who planned the Rover strategy for peacetime, and by the start of 1945 he already knew what he wanted to do. Clearly remembering how the car market had behaved in the years immediately after the 1914–1918 war, he had decided on a two-pronged strategy. On the one hand, Rover should get back into business by resuming production of their pre-war saloon models. On the other hand, he anticipated the same sort of interest in less expensive models as had become evident in the early 1920s, and he believed that Rover should offer an economy model alongside the traditional saloons.

As Maurice Wilks explained it to Harold Hastings for a feature article in *The Motor* of 10 August 1949:

> *It appeared to us that there would be a big demand for economy. It seemed plain that petrol would remain short for some years and that this would automatically create a large market for small-engined cars with low fuel consumption.... Our idea was that there would ... be scope for a really small quality car which would appeal to people who had run more-expensive types in the past and wished to retain the same standards, even if economy of running forced them to use much smaller vehicles.*

At the Board meeting on 18 January 1945, S. B. Wilks formally proposed to his colleagues that Rover should introduce a new 6hp car. He believed that this could sell at a rate of 5,000 a year, a figure he portrayed as an increase over the numbers of more traditional saloons that the company might build. The Board were in complete agreement with this strategy, although it certainly represented a quite radical step for Rover.

By comparison with the traditional Rover models that began with a 10hp and went on up to a 20hp, a 6hp car was in a completely different category. A 6hp model would be smaller than anything Rover had made since 1912, when the company was still becoming established as a car maker. Even the aborted Scarab model of 1931

Pictured at the Solihull factory, probably in 1946, this was one of the running prototypes of the M Model...

... and this is probably the same car, seen from behind. The boot shape deliberately resembled that of the larger Rovers then in production.

had been planned as a 7hp, and the successful air-cooled model of the early 1920s had been an 8hp.

By the time Wilks secured the agreement of his colleagues to proceed, the Rover engineers had already done a good deal of work on the new 6hp. They had also obtained for examination and evaluation a Fiat 500, the remarkable little Italian car that had been introduced in 1936 and had sold quite well in Britain. The company's Chief Draughtsman, Roland Seale, was preparing drawings of some of its components by early 1945.

Not that Rover ever intended to make anything so crude as a copy of the little Fiat. Whatever they built would be made to Rover standards, even if it was small, and of course Chief Engineer Maurice Wilks probably saw it as a good opportunity to experiment with some new ideas. It must also have been his idea to call it the M Model; the M presumably stood for Miniature. Some documents call it Model M, and at that 1949 interview for *The Motor*, he also called it the M1.

Structure

The car that came together during 1945 and the first half of 1946 was certainly unconventional, and probably incorporated a lot of ideas from chassis designer Gordon Bashford as well as from a young Norwegian engineer named Scott Iverson, who was an original thinker but did not remain with Rover for long after the war ended.

In fact, the M Model would not have a conventional chassis at all but would be built up on a light-alloy 'platform' consisting of the floor and the front bulkhead, with a forward projection to accommodate the engine, gearbox and front suspension. The transmission tunnel would provide the main longitudinal stiffening and there would be box-section stiffeners to give additional strength. The body, too, was going to be of lightweight aluminium alloy, and although various different alloys were under consideration, the favoured supplier in November 1945 seemed to be Northern Aluminium – presumably the company then based at Newport in Monmouthshire that later became Noral and subsequently part of Alcan. There is no indication, by the way, that the Birmabright aluminium alloy later chosen for the Land-Rover was among the options considered for the M Model.

One document dated 19 November 1945 shows that the weight of the chassis (specified as being without the body, and presumably including axles but not the powertrain) was estimated at 738lb (roughly 335kg, or just over 6.5cwt). The overall weight of the prototype that Harold Hastings of *The Motor* drove in 1949 was quoted as 13.5cwt (1,512lb or about 686kg).

As for dimensions, the wheelbase was 77 inches, which compares with the 78.75 inches of the Fiat 500. The prototypes would be 136 inches (3,455mm) long, 56 inches (1,422mm) wide and 55 inches (1,397mm) tall. The M Model had independent front suspension (which would not reach a production Rover until the P3 of 1948), a 'live' rear axle located by radius arms and a Panhard rod, and coil springs all round. The steering was a worm and nut type, giving a turning circle of 28ft 6in on the prototypes, and the wheels were 14-inch steel discs running with 4.75 × 14 tyres.

Engine and Gearbox

Rover were already intending that their new post-war engine range should have the inlet-over-exhaust configuration that chief engine designer Jack Swaine had drawn up before the war, but it was obvious that all the versions under consideration for the full-size Rovers were physically too large for the M Model. Work therefore began on a much smaller derivative, a four-cylinder engine with dimensions dictated by the RAC formula that determined the fiscal horsepower rating. The new 6hp engine ended up with a swept volume of just 699cc.

Surviving documents include a preliminary engine specification that must have been prepared in late 1944 (the document is dated

The engine was a 699cc size, using the new Rover IOE design.

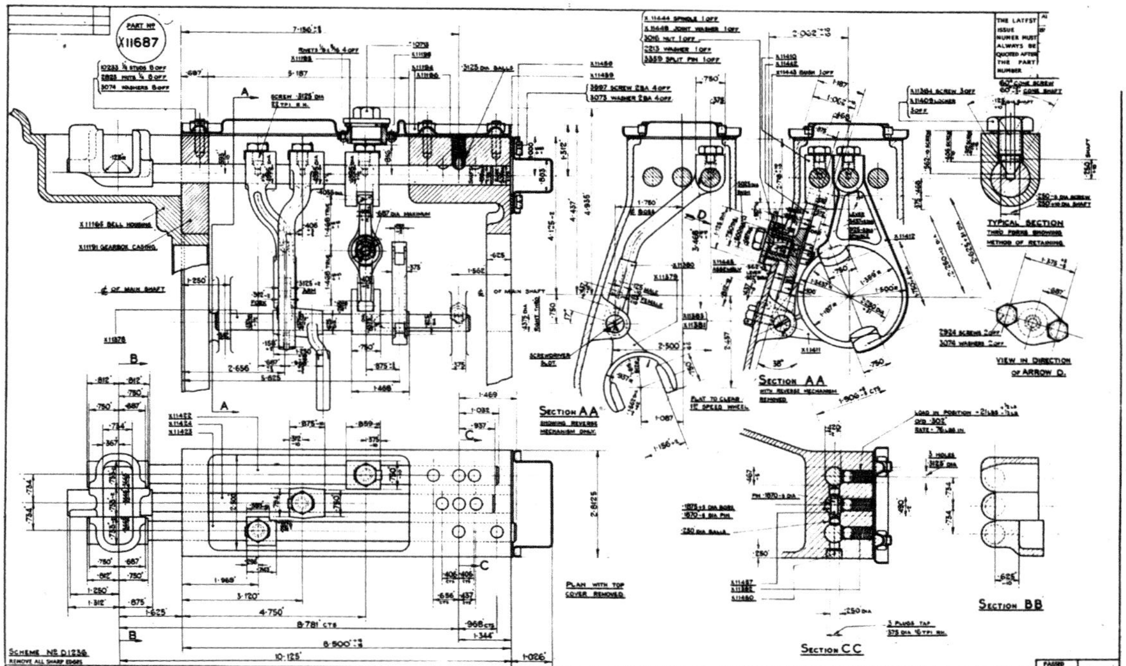

This engineering drawing is dated 22 November 1945 and shows the planned four-speed gearbox. Its number, X11687, shows that it was considered experimental at this stage.

10 January 1945). This shows that the engine was to be extremely short, with a length of just 19.375 inches between the front face of the fan and the rear face of the cylinder block. The planned dimensions included a 57mm bore and a 68.5mm stroke, and the block was to be designed to allow for a longer 73mm stroke, so that the engine could easily be enlarged to 745cc at a later date. There were to be alternative 8:1 and 9:1 compression ratios, but the experimental engines would all be high-compression types.

This engine was expected to deliver 28.5bhp at 5,000rpm and 37lb ft of torque at 2,300rpm. The figures sound puny, but to make it all work the M Model was to be as light as possible. With a 4.57:1 axle ratio, the car was expected to give the same performance (that is, presumably, acceleration) as a Rover Sixteen, and with a 3.94:1 axle for better fuel economy, it would accelerate as well as a 1939 Twelve. Performance was certainly not going to be shabby; this was, after all, to be a Rover as well as a miniature car.

Roland Seale drew up the four-speed gearbox during 1945, and by the time the prototypes were built this was operated by a push-pull gearchange broadly similar to that used on the Citroën Traction Avant. The main reason for this was that the gearbox would not be in its conventional location under the floor between the front seats but much further forward. The engine itself was going to be mounted ahead of the front wheel centre-line – a design feature that may well have been inspired by the layout of the Fiat 500.

A Matter of Appearance

At that interview with Harold Hastings for *The Motor* feature in late summer 1949, Maurice Wilks produced a pair of early scale models for the M Model that he said had been made in 1945. These certainly suggest that the original plan for the car was quite unconventional, the earlier one being an open two-seater roadster with styling that would have been very advanced indeed for the time. The later one used the same basic hull, but with the addition of a fixed coupé roof.

Both models had a long nose in front of the passenger compartment, and within that nose were two distinct compartments. Perhaps the plan was to put the luggage 'boot' ahead of the passengers, though whether the engine would have been ahead of it or behind it is something we may never know. Equally possible is that the two-compartment design simply reflects the idea later adopted on prototypes of a separate compartment behind the engine to house the battery, tools and other items.

These scale models made in 1945 show early thinking about Rover's small economy car.

One way or another, those original plans had been abandoned by July 1945. A new 1/16 scale model was made that month, presumably from wood and plasticene, and this was very clearly a two-door saloon along the lines of the Fiat. Its protruding boot broadly resembled that on full-size Rovers, and its front end carried an upright grille. In many ways, it was a shrunken version of the pre-war saloons that Rover were preparing to put back into production. By the time the prototypes were built – and quite possibly at this stage in mid-1945 – the car had also turned into a 2+2, with rear seats that offered just about enough room for a pair of children.

'Model M, Design no1' was turned into a full-size mock-up during August 1945, but there was clearly some hesitation about the front-end details because the two sides had different headlamp treatments. Maurice Wilks seems not to have been happy with either of them, and later that month the front end of the mock-up (or perhaps a second mock-up) was modified to reflect Design no2. This gave the whole car a much wider appearance by moving the lamps out to the wing fronts and by using a horizontal radiator grille in place of the traditional vertical Rover type.

September was then a busy month, with no fewer than four more front-end designs being tried out on the full-size mock-up. Design no3 differed from its predecessor mainly in a larger bonnet panel, which would have given better access to the engine. Design no4 brought the headlamps inboard again and then Design no5 had a rather uncomfortably notched front to the bonnet. Design no6 moved the headlamps down

This 1/16 scale model, apparently made of wood and plasticene, dates from July 1945.

Now translated to a full-size model, this was the state of play in August 1945. It was described as Design no 1.

Design no 2, also from August 1945, shows an alternative approach to the front-end styling.

A third design mock-up had minor front end differences from the second one. This was dated September 1945.

More work on the front end produced Design no 4 in September.

Design no 5 followed later the same month, adding a different kind of definition to the front end.

Yet another attempt in September 1945 produced Design no 6. This model did not have alternative proposals on different sides; other pictures show that the grille bars not visible on the far side here were in fact present.

For Design no 7 in October 1945, there clearly were different proposals on each side of the mock-up. The grille badge reads 'Rover 12' and was obviously used only to give an idea of the finished appearance.

Design no 8, again from October 1945, had a really radical proposal for the headlamp positions. A similar design would be used on the Model P mock-up a month later.

The boxy sections around the headlamps on Design no 9 from December 1945 were an early iteration of the style eventually adopted for the P4 – and for the Model M prototypes.

and alongside the horizontal radiator grille, resulting in a front end that looked a lot like that of the 1948 Morris Minor!

Still Maurice Wilks was not satisfied, and October brought seventh and eighth designs. The earlier one had a narrower but still horizontal grille, with two alternative headlamp positions; the later one went completely radical with the headlamps concealed behind a glass panel in the nose of the bonnet above another narrow horizontal grille.

Finally, in November and December 1945, Design no9 brought a satisfactory result. The grille became an inverted T shape, so combining the best of both horizontal and vertical designs, and the headlamps were fitted behind glass covers into the notches of the T. It was this design that was carried forward to the running prototypes.

Prototypes

We know relatively little about the prototypes, but we do know from an entry in Rover's photographic ledger that pictures of a 'light car' mock-up were taken for Maurice Wilks on 21 August 1946. The pictures themselves have not so far surfaced, although it is not beyond the bounds of possibility that some or all of the undated pictures printed here (which came from Gordon Bashford in 1985) belong to that set.

That date of August 1946 is quite late for Rover to have been still working with a mock-up, and it seems very likely that this was a final stage before the construction of prototypes. We do not know exactly how many prototypes were built, but the figure of six has been suggested. From the traces that have been uncovered over the years, it seems more likely that there were fewer than that – perhaps no more than two or three.

One of those prototypes was registered as FNX 799. The FNX series was first issued in November 1946, so this would suggest that the car was put on the road in November or December 1946. The prototype that Harold Hastings drove in 1949 wore trade plates for the photographs, so we cannot tell if it was the same car or a different one. However, it has no very obvious differences from FNX 799. Legend has it that works director Jess Worster used an M Model prototype as his everyday transport until the late 1950s or early 1960s, but we do not know its registration number. Worster would have used that car on condition that he could not sell it on but had to return it to the Rover Company when he no longer wanted it, and there is no doubt that it would eventually have been broken up.

The prototypes, then, must have been constructed at the end of 1946 and into the early months of 1947, actually at a time when Britain was experiencing one of its worst winters on record. At about this time, it was also becoming apparent that the post-war car-buying public did not want economy cars at all but wanted proper cars to reassure themselves that all was well with the world again.

The Bigger Picture

It is important to see all this design and development work in context, of course. However much enthusiasm design engineers like Maurice Wilks and Gordon Bashford were able to muster, their

This fascinating but undated picture shows some styling work on a panelled body, which quite likely belonged to one of the running prototypes. The front support was presumably necessary to support the weight of the lengthened front end.

This mock-up was produced to try out the engineering layout, and the two scaffolding poles visible were purely structural!

dreams were severely constrained by the conditions in post-war Britain.

There was also the simple matter of paying for it all, and on 16 September 1946 S. B. Wilks told the Rover Board that new capital was required to fund the production of the new small car (he did not call it the M Model). A month later, he advised them that setting a date for the start of production had now become even more difficult in view of a shortage of steel. American supplies of sheet steel had now ceased, and the British government was intending to introduce a new rationing scheme for such supplies as were available. Wilks of course intended to visit the ministry to lobby for increased supplies to Rover – but all those present must have realised that his voice would be just one among many from manufacturing industry and that there was no reason to believe Rover would be accorded special treatment.

These problems remained unresolved during the first half of 1947, and continuing work on the prototype M Models was done amid shortages of materials and in the face of government insistence on prioritising exports. Severe power cuts reduced production, and by May

The underbonnet layout was not quite as predicted on the engineering mock-up! Of interest is the two-compartment design, with the battery and fluid reservoirs located away from the engine.

Rover were working a four-day week on alternate weeks. It must have been during this period, too, that the whole concept of the M Model began to be called into question. Both at home and abroad there was a discernible reluctance to accept small cars; buyers wanted large, modern cars to express their exuberance at the return of peace, and the market that S. B. Wilks had envisaged for the M Model had simply not materialised. The M Model did not fit the bill.

In the meantime, Maurice Wilks had become convinced that Rover should improve its chances of export sales by building a light 4 × 4 runabout similar to the wartime Jeep. Preliminary work on this concept probably took some resources away from the M Model project over the summer of 1947, and by the early autumn, the project was effectively dead. On 4 September, the Rover Board approved production of the vehicle that would be launched in April 1948 as the Land-Rover, and the M Model faded from the picture.

CHAPTER 4

Frustration: The Road to P3

When Rover decided to re-start production of its pre-war models in order to get back into the car market in 1945, nobody was under any illusion that this should be more than a temporary measure. It was simply expedient – and it was a course of action that several other British car makers followed at the time. They had been prevented from developing new models during the war years, and so they had to get back into the game with old ones. But from the moment they began to contemplate their post-war future, each and every one of them knew that they needed new designs as quickly as possible.

At Rover, a new engine design had been under development when war broke out in 1939, and it was obvious that this should be revived and carried through to production. There were also new thoughts about chassis design, and the same applied to these. Chapter 3 explains more about how the technical elements of the new post-war Rovers came together. There was obviously going to be a third major element in any new design, of course, and that was the body. The difficulty of creating an acceptable new design became a major hindrance to progress at Rover, and a solution was not found until mid-1946.

Car body design had changed in leaps and bounds in the time since the current Rover design had been introduced in autumn 1936. The traditional designs with separate wings and running-boards were beginning to look distinctly old-fashioned alongside new full-width 'envelope' bodies – although this was not a particularly pressing problem for Rover, because their clientele tended to conservative tastes.

American designs had reached Britain during the war years as staff cars with the US military stationed here, and were offering a radically different appearance. Even in Europe there were signs of change. Opel's remarkable Kadett of 1935 had introduced a new approach to the lower end of the market, and had swiftly been copied by Renault as the Juvaquatre a couple of years later. At the top end of the market, European coachbuilders had also begun to produce some extraordinarily attractive designs that indicated the way ahead.

Maurice Wilks was clearly well aware of these changes. The evidence of his attempts to create a pleasing new style for the eventual new full-size Rover is contained in a series of carefully dated photographs pasted into an album. Alongside these are photographs of his attempts

Maurice Wilks knew what he wanted as early as July 1945, as this scale model of a possible Rover 20 makes clear.

to create a pleasing style for the M Model (*see* Chapter 3), which he was working on at the same time. Themes and ideas are sometimes shared between the two, but it is possible to focus on the full-size car alone and to trace the progress of its design. No doubt there was input from Ben Loker, too, who was Rover's chief body designer and would have worked closely with Wilks on any new design.

The earliest pictures of the full-size Rover are dated July 1945, and show a scale model, probably made of wood and plasticene, that is described as 'Proposed new saloon'. It is described as being in 1/16th scale, so it must have been about a foot long, and it carries the number-plate ROV 20, which suggests it was intended as a top-of-the-range 20hp type. What is quite remarkable about it is that it does not look like any earlier Rover at all. It has a full-width body with shallow wing projections around the wheelarches that suggest the influence of the pre-war Opel and Renault designs, and it has a full-width front end with the headlights integrated into the body panels and a horizontal radiator grille that suggests American influence. The two-pane vee screen may have been inspired by American designs, too; existing Rovers had single-piece windscreens.

By the standards of 1945, it was quite radical, and Maurice Wilks probably realised that it went too far to appeal to Rover's typically discreet and conservative clientele. None of his subsequent designs for the new post-war saloon were derived from it. However, he clearly did not give up on these early thoughts. When he came to design the next generation of Rover saloons (which became the P4 range in 1949), the head-

A new approach to front end styling was introduced in Europe by the Opel Kadett of 1935. This seems to have had some influence on early designs for the P3.

lamps were built into box-like panels that quite obviously came from the same line of thought as that 1945 model.

November–December 1945

It may be that Wilks also had some reservations about whether such a radically new body could be built at the time. There certainly were shortages of skilled men in 1945, and there was no immediate hope of these ending; many former Rover men had been killed in the fighting, and others were stranded in far-off countries awaiting release from military duties. Rover already had a relationship with Pressed Steel, but that company was likely to be facing the same problems, and

Trying to add a modern full-width front end to the existing Rover body design proved a challenge too far. These two pictures are dated November and December 1945.

there was no doubt that its services would soon be in unprecedented demand as other car makers returned to business.

The upshot of this was that Wilks decided to retain as much as possible of the existing Rover body and to modernise its appearance with a full-width front end. In order to do this, he appears to have started with a full-size six-light saloon bodyshell that was cut in half length-ways and widened (the partially-disguised join is clearly visible in pictures). He then modified its appearance to get what he wanted – or, at least, he instructed his assistants to do so. As modeller's clay had not yet reached Britain, the modifications were almost certainly made with plasticene and the photographs bear witness to the difficulty of getting a completely smooth surface with this material. All of them seem to have been taken in a corner of the main building at Solihull, which had presumably been designated as the Mock-Up Shop.

Three photographs of this first full-size mock-up exist, all described in the album simply as 'Proposed new car'. The first two are dated November 1945 and the third December 1945, and by that date the mock-up had acquired the dummy registration plate EVC 301. The full-width front has a quite extraordinary design, with pontoon-like front wings, a horizontal radiator grille, and square headlamps. The whole thing has been added around a standard-looking engine compartment, leaving a strange aperture where the top of a standard Rover grille would have been situated. This has been filled in with a slightly bizarre feature that may have been intended as either a fog or passing lamp. Meanwhile, the bumper was very American in appearance, and the whole style had some echoes of the late-1930s' 'coffin-nose' Cord 810.

December 1945: Model P3

Unsurprisingly, Maurice Wilks seems to have rejected that design and to have started again. Photographs from December 1945 show that the next design still wore the EVC 301 registration plate, so the new front end may well have been grafted onto the older mock-up. This time, the legend in the photographic album describes the picture as 'Model P3.'

There could be all sorts of reasons for this choice of name. It could perhaps stand for 'Proposal 3'. The first Proposal would have been the July 1945 1/16th-scale model; the second would have been the one with the Cord-like front end; and this one would have been the third. However, later models are simply described as 'Model P', and a more likely explanation is that the P stood for 'Post-War'. Rover had not used model codes of this type before the war but they suddenly appeared in the late 1940s: J (Jeep) indicated the Land-Rover and T indicated the (Gas) Turbine cars.

If P stood for Post-War, the number 3 then requires a different explanation. A strong possibility (based on logic rather than evidence) is that the M Model was thought of as number 1, the revived pre-war cars were considered to be number 2, and as the third in the post-war series, the new saloon was number 3. Maurice Wilks certainly did refer to the M Model as the M1, as Chapter 3 explains, and the revived pre-war cars were sometimes described as P2 types. Other explanations may be possible: suffice it to say that this note in the photographic album is the first known use of the P3 internal model code that was adopted for the 1948 Rovers.

This December 1945 proposal has a less extraordinary front end than its predecessor, this time with round headlamps (in square panels) and a grille that is less aggressively horizontal. A similar arrangement was tried on the M Model and was retained for the prototypes. The strange American-style bumper is still present, and pictures of the mock-up from other angles show that although it looks comfortingly like the existing production Rovers, the front end does not blend in well with the overall lines.

This was the first mock-up described as Model P3. The pictures date from December 1945.

January–February 1946: Model P

The next iteration of the styling was simply called Model P in the photograph album and had a much softer and more rounded front-end style, with a short radiator grille bearing the established triangular Rover badge, and what was probably a standard production bumper. The headlights were now mounted in volumes that joined the wings to the sides of the engine compartment and the grille. This one was 'registered' as ROV 22.

That was January's effort. Meanwhile, as we know from the Rover Board minutes of September 1946, a plan had been drawn up to make the new engines available for the 1947 season (which would begin in October) by putting them into the existing Sports Saloons. That was abandoned over the summer because serious shortages were still affecting manufacturing industry and Rover had to focus on simply keeping going as best it could. Nevertheless, one photograph in the album of body designs suggests that a prototype may have been built, with a slightly modified front end design.

The photograph is dated February 1946 and almost certainly shows a real car, with a steering wheel and windscreen wipers and a real front axle that is visible under its revised frontal treatment. The front wings have been reworked to frame a shorter radiator grille, which is painted rather than chromed (no doubt an expedient to overcome the periodic shortages of chrome plate that affected the motor industry at the time). There are free-standing headlamps in the traditional

A squat radiator surround and a deep valance produced this more attractive design in January 1946, but Maurice Wilks was not satisfied.

This much more resolved design is dated February 1946, and picks up on the squat radiator and deep valance of the previous one. Perhaps plans for a more radical front end were at least on hold. This looks very much like a real car, but if it is, what are those wooden body supports just behind the steering wheel?

Back to those full-width front end designs again… this is 'ROV 22' from February 1946, and mock-ups with that 'registration' probably remained in use until September.

manner, and there is also a deep front valance, which carries a centrally-mounted auxiliary lamp – exactly the sort of thing that might have been prepared for a Sports Saloon, and an interesting precursor of the design eventually adopted for the P3 models. The grille badge reads 'Rover 16', but of course that does not prove that the car had a 16hp engine!

Still focusing on the eventual replacement model, Maurice Wilks nevertheless made yet another attempt to achieve a satisfactory style in February 1946. The ROV 22 mock-up received yet another new front end that incorporated some of the grille and headlamp ideas tried earlier on 'EVC 301'. It was still far from successful, however, and it may have been Wilks' last attempt to graft pontoon wings and a new front end onto the widened pre-war body. It is certainly the last new design in the album of photographs, and the last one to be described as Model P.

Summer 1946: the Change of Plan

The ROV 22 mock-up seems to have remained in use for a few more months, but we know this only from a catalogue of company photographs, and neither negatives nor any prints seem to have survived. The later pictures are in three sets. The first is dated 23 May 1946 and shows the ROV 22 'mock-up in plasticene'; one of the three pictures is described as showing the rear wing, which suggests some design changes had been made there. The second set is dated 14 June and is simply described as 'mock-up of car'; it is certainly not a mock-up of the M Model, because a further set of pictures was catalogued for this. The four pictures focus on the front end, so this sounds like a further continuation of Wilks' experiments with a revised frontal appearance. The third set, dated 3 September 1946, again contains three pictures. It is described as 'R.22 mock-up', which is almost certainly ROV 22 again.

It is not hard to imagine Maurice Wilks becoming increasingly frustrated with his attempts to design a satisfactory new body, and becoming increasingly aware too that other car makers were pressing ahead with their plans for new post-war models while Rover seemed to be held up. However, it must have been over the summer of 1946 that Wilks saw the first pictures of the new 1947-model Studebakers and realised that their revolutionary 'three-box' styling would provide the body design answers he wanted.

He would also have recognised that a new body along those lines would take some time to prepare. So it must have been in the late summer or early autumn of 1946 that he decided to go for an interim model with the new chassis and engines under a widened version of the existing body. The idea of reducing the size of the Rover model range was also in the air by this stage, and S. B. Wilks raised what he called the issue of standardisation at the August 1946 Board meeting. The idea was to follow the guidelines suggested by the Ministry of Supply that still controlled the allocation of raw materials and to create a new range of cars that had just one chassis and two engines.

So it was that the P3 project was effectively divided into two. On the one hand, the new mechanical elements would be clothed in a revised body of traditional style to give Rover a short-term model that they hoped would enter production for the 1948 season. This would retain the P3 name. On the other, further-developed versions of those new mechanical elements under a new body that incorporated the latest styling ideas would create a second new model called P4, which Rover would put into production as soon as they reasonably could.

CHAPTER 5

Evolution: 'One of Britain's Fine Cars – Now Made Finer!'

By the late summer of 1946, the plans for the cars that would be introduced as the Rover P3 range in early 1948 seem to have been fairly well established. Work on the modernised pre-war bodyshell mock-ups had ceased some months earlier, and the intention was now to use an improved and widened bodyshell of traditional appearance, a new box-section chassis of the type under development before the war, and the new sloping-head engine that had also been under development at the end of the 1930s. Independent front suspension must have been in the plan, too, and the earliest evidence of its development is some photographs dated August 1946.

The new range of cars would also be slimmer than the old. The existing range consisted of seven models – Saloons on the four-cylinder 10hp and 12hp, and the six-cylinder 14hp and 16hp chassis, and Sports Saloons on the 12hp, 14hp and 16hp. The new range would consist of just four models, which would be Saloons and Sports Saloons on a single four-cylinder (12hp) chassis and a single six-cylinder (16hp) chassis. At the Board meeting in August 1946, managing director S. B. Wilks raised the question of one chassis with two engines, and referred to 'standardisation'. While this was certainly a sensible policy on its own merits, that reference to standardisation does suggest that Rover had been influenced by the Board of Trade's call for greater standardisation in manufacturing industry to help increase production.

In September 1946, Wilks informed the Board that he hoped the new P3 models would be available in time for the October 1947 motor show. It was a forlorn hope: no motor show would be held in 1947, and the inevitable delays caused the car's development timetable to slip. In December 1946, Wilks told his fellow directors that there were difficulties in obtaining the necessary dies and tools for the planned 1948 models, and by the time of the July 1947 Board meeting, he was hoping that production would begin in early 1948. He also highlighted the key features of the planned new cars as independent front suspension, the new sloping-head engine, and wider bodies. Each one of those elements deserves consideration here.

Engine

The origins of the new sloping-head engine could be traced to 1936, when Maurice Wilks asked his engine designer Jack Swaine to draw up a V6 engine. His idea was that this would be

Early advertising for the P3 stressed 'the traditional smoothness and refinements associated with Rover cars, plus a new responsiveness.' The car illustrated has the four-light body, which looked less dated than the six-light type, and the country house in the background suggests luxurious living.

no longer than an in-line four-cylinder and could therefore fit under a bonnet of the same length. Using a V6 instead of a straight-six would avoid the need for Rover to produce chassis of two different lengths while offering both four- and six-cylinder models.

Swaine's first design showed promise, but it was his second design in 1938 that bore fruit. This had the inlet valves in the cylinder heads while the exhaust valves were in the block on the outside of the vee. To minimise the engine's width so that it would fit under the narrow bonnets of

The new F-head or IOE engines were central to the P3, and one is seen here with its gearbox attached. Their combustion chamber design was ideally suited to the poor quality of post-war 'pool' petrol.

Chassis and drivetrain of a six-cylinder P3 are seen here on a trolley alongside the assembly track. A close look reveals that the frame side-members end some distance ahead of the rear axle.

This press advertisement blank from June 1948 shows the four-light and six-light bodies together, and adds the new strap-line: 'One of Britain's Fine Cars – now made finer!'.

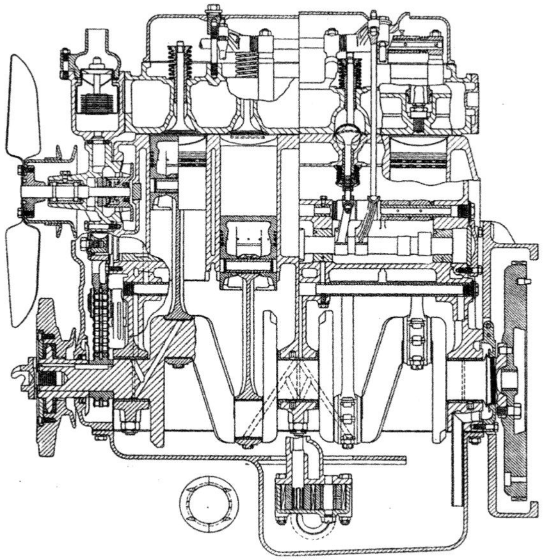

This engineering drawing shows the layout of the four-cylinder engine in the 60.

the late-1930s Rovers, Swaine tipped the face of each cylinder head towards the centre of the engine, so creating a 'sloping head' design. From this came a wedge-shaped combustion chamber, in which he placed the spark plug centrally. This gave excellent test results and, even though the V6 itself was abandoned, towards the end of 1938 Maurice Wilks asked Swaine to incorporate

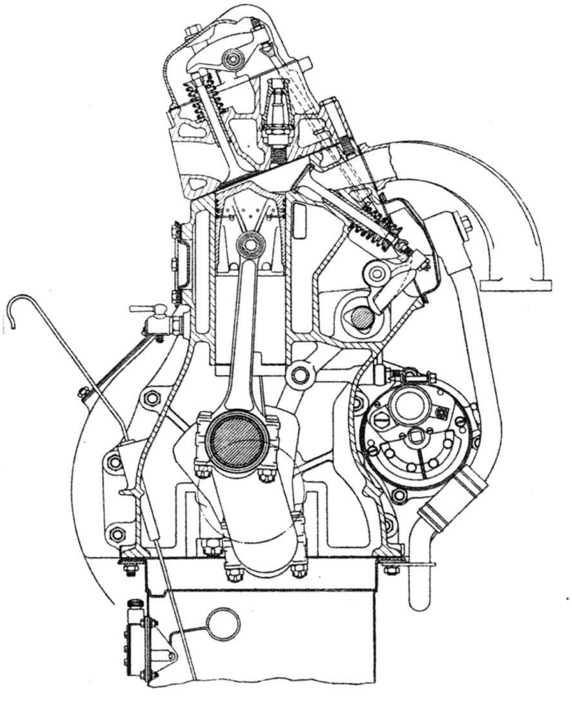

This drawing shows the layout of the engine, as seen from the front.

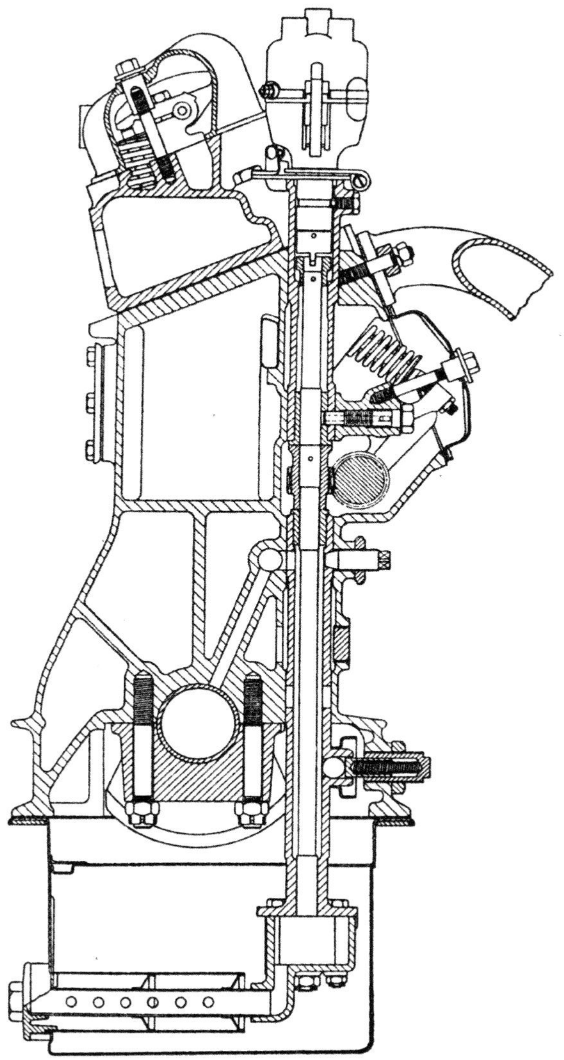

Again seen from the front of the engine, this cross-section of the cylinder block shows other aspects of its layout.

the combustion chamber design into the next generation of Rover's in-line four-cylinder and six-cylinder engines. These engines were under development as war broke out in 1939.

Unsurprisingly, Swaine drew up different versions of the engine to replace the various sizes that Rover then had in production. The four-cylinders were drawn up as 10hp and 12hp types, and research by Kevin Shearman suggests that there were two or three prototypes of the smaller engine and four of the larger one. The six-cylinder was drawn up as a 14hp and a 16hp, and surviving records suggest that there were at least three 14hp engines and at least four 16hp prototypes. Interestingly, there does not appear to have been a 20hp size to replace Rover's largest pre-war engine – but the sloping-head design was further adapted to make the little 6hp engine intended for the M Model. This was the only member of the family that did not have a stroke of 105mm.

What we know for sure is that Rover claimed the six-cylinder engine had done 600,000 test miles either on the road or on the bench by the time it entered production in 1948. As for the four-cylinder, one prototype engine was fitted into a prototype box-section frame that was given the body of a Rover Ten. Registered DDU 588 in February 1938, this car is said to have been used throughout the war years by Maurice Wilks. Once its time as a development vehicle was over, the car was dismantled and used as the basis of the Rover Special single-seater racing car that Spen King and colleagues built in 1948.

Rover's decision to limit the P3 range to one four-cylinder and one six-cylinder model meant that two of the proposed engine sizes would not go forward to production. The 10hp and 14hp sizes were therefore abandoned, while the 1,595cc 12hp and 2,103cc 16hp types remained in the programme. However, the designations 12hp and 16hp were never used on the production cars because the old RAC horsepower taxation system was abandoned at the start of 1947. Instead, the new cars were given names that reflected (if only approximately) their engine's output in real horsepower. So the 12hp became a 60 and the 16hp became a 75.

Rover always described these new engines as sloping-head types, and prototype examples were numbered with an SH prefix code to identify them. In more recent years, they have tended to be known as IOE types (the letters stand for Inlet Over Exhaust) because of the layout of their valves. Now that the IOE layout has been superseded by more efficient designs, it is easy to forget just how advanced these engines were for their time, as well as how much they were praised by the motoring press back in 1948. The sloping-head design not only gave very good economy, but it also coped extremely well with the low-quality 72-octane 'Pool' petrol that was the only sort available in Britain in the late 1940s. These engines were also remarkably quiet in operation when maintained to their maker's specifications.

Chassis

The idea of using box-section frame members to make a rigid chassis had been proposed by Adrian Lombard, a Rover engineer who worked on the jet engine project during the war and then went with that project to Rolls-Royce. Gordon Bashford, who actually designed the P3 chassis, was always most insistent on crediting Lombard with the idea. Rover had recognised that they needed a more rigid chassis frame as long ago as 1934, when they had been forced to abandon the independent front suspension (IFS) planned and advertised for the 1935 Speed Fourteen models. Bashford remembered that the channel-section frame then in use twisted too much for the IFS to work properly.

With an appropriately stiff chassis frame, Rover could go for IFS again on the new post-war car. By August 1946, an experimental system was on test, and captions on surviving pictures show that it was intended for Model P – the new full-size Rover. A rather simpler system was eventually adopted for production, but those pictures bear witness to Rover's intentions and put a date on them.

The next key characteristic of the new chassis was a Gordon Bashford idea. He knew that existing Rovers had their chassis frames underslung (that is, below the axle and springs) at the rear because this allowed the body to be mounted lower and so reduced the overall height of the car. He also knew that the underslung frame

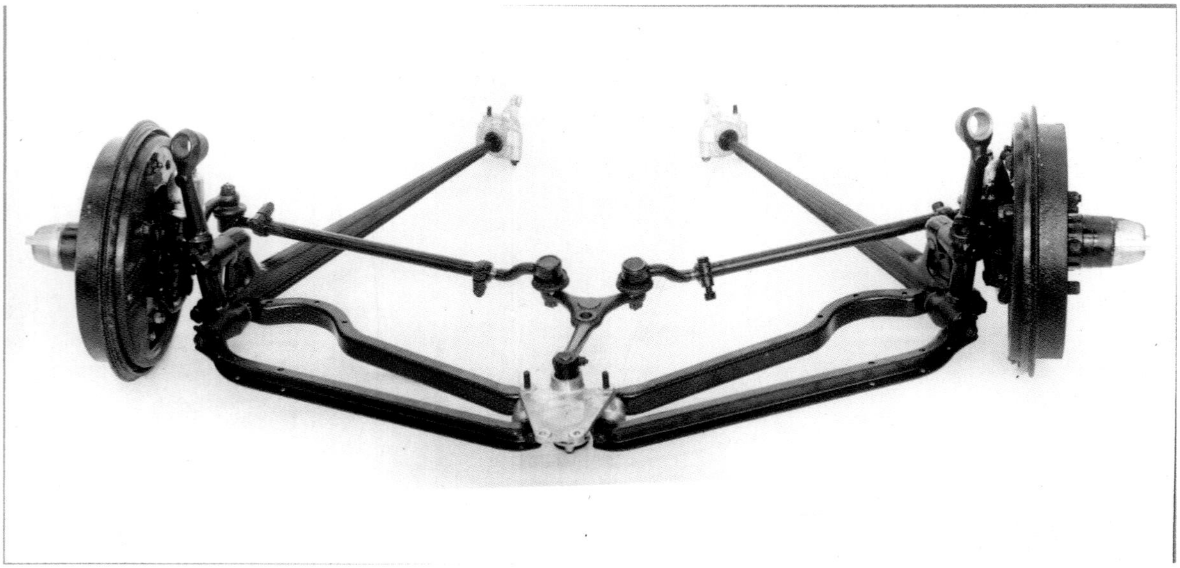

This interesting view shows the layout of the early P3 independent front suspension and steering. The coil springs were mounted to the outer ends of the lower arms, which look surprisingly flimsy, and an anti-roll bar ran between the loops visible at the top of the suspension uprights.

limited suspension travel. So, he reasoned, why not avoid having a chassis frame at the rear altogether, thus allowing for lower overall height and giving full suspension travel at the same time?

His P3 chassis design therefore had side members that reached only to the front mountings of the rear springs. Behind that, the all-steel bodywork carried the stresses, and a tubular cross-member attached to the underside of the body served as an anchorage point for the rear ends of the springs. As an engineer's solution, it was logical and clever; it would only be many years later, when rust began to eat away at the rear of the bodies, that its disadvantage would become apparent.

Using IFS also meant that rod-operated brakes were no longer practicable for the front axle. So Rover switched to a hybrid system, retaining rod operation for the rear brakes but using hydraulic brakes at the front. A front anti-roll bar ensured that the new suspension's compliance did not upset the handling on corners, and new Burman Douglas recirculating-ball steering incorporated a variable ratio for the first time on a Rover. Other modern features, much appreciated when the P3s were new, included sealed-for-life joints and rubber bushes in the suspension, which together reduced the need for regular greasing.

Bodies

The revived pre-war Rovers had been made available with two different body styles, a four-light Sports Saloon and a more upright but closely related six-light Saloon. For the P3, Rover planned to offer the same two styles, although perhaps because of the sobriety of the times the Sports Saloon designation was dropped: instead, sales catalogues referred to four-light and six-light saloon bodies.

Nevertheless, the P3 bodies were much more different from those of the cars they replaced than a casual glance would suggest. Most importantly, perhaps, they were no longer composite types with metal panels and wooden frame members, but were all-steel constructions stamped out by Pressed Steel and assembled at Solihull. They were some 2.5 inches wider than before, which gave more room inside. The passenger compartment was also 5 inches further forward, mainly in the interests of better weight distribution. The bonnet was shorter, too, and was the same length whether it housed a four-cylinder or a six-cylinder engine. A broader radiator grille and a single central pass-lamp gave the P3s a distinctive appearance from the front, while tail lights on the wings and new over-riders made them easy to recognise from the rear.

Pictured within the grounds of the Solihull factory, this early six-light model displays its sliding sunroof. It does not appear to have had the fine lining applied to the body sides.

The four-light body is seen here on a late 1948 75 model. The red reflectors on the quarter-bumpers were not on the cars when new, but were required after a change in UK lighting regulations in 1954.

The neat and discreet interior had the gear lever set between individual front seats, and a dashboard of traditional Rover design but modified to make room for a radio. The one fitted is a Radiomobile 100 set, and the control immediately below it is for the freewheel.

The rear compartment of a six-light saloon model shows the armrests that gave the design so much character – and yet it was a design that was already looking old-fashioned. Behind the seat back is another traditional feature: a rear window blind that could be pulled up by a cord accessible to the driver.

This underbonnet picture of a 75 shows the six-cylinder engine with its large air cleaner. The built-in heater that was an important advance for the P3 is at the rear of the picture on the left. The washer bottle was not an original feature, but was fitted later to meet new regulations.

The extra width was quite noticeable inside the cars, but perhaps most important for many customers was that the bodies had a heating and ventilating system built in as standard. This removed the need for an opening windscreen, so the P3's screen was fixed in place. An air slot below the base of the screen helped with demisting and defrosting (although by modern standards it was pretty ineffective), while heat reached the front footwells through a Clayton Dewandre unit that was plumbed into the engine's cooling system.

An air duct running alongside the engine delivered ambient air from the front of the car to the ventilating system, and warm air could be circulated by means of an electric blower motor. So there was hardly ever a need to open the windows while travelling – but if the windows were opened, louvres over the drop-glasses would prevent rain from dripping into the passenger compartment, just as they had on the P2 bodies. The driver's window could be raised quickly by means of a quick-lift lever mechanism, and the familiar Rover sliding roof was also standard.

The dashboard followed the established Rover pattern, with its instruments placed centrally, but had been redesigned to accommodate the optional radio, which on the 1947 models was mounted below it. A radio was still very much a luxury item in 1948. Rover offered an HMV set, which was of course a large and cumbersome valve type, and fitted its speaker to the roof just above the windscreen, where it could best be heard.

Despite the austerity and restrictions of the late 1940s, there were also plans for a Drophead Coupé body. This would not be made by Pressed

Steel, but would be a low-volume hand-built body along the lines of the elegant drophead coupés made by Salmons & Sons on the Rovers of the late 1930s. Salmons & Sons, now known as Tickford after their best-known design, were asked to produce a design during 1948 and built two prototypes – although no production followed.

The P3 Prototypes

There is no indication that a 10hp P3 prototype was ever built, but there were definitely prototypes of 12hp, 14hp and 16hp variants. The 14hp would not go forward to production, but the 12hp and 16hp would go on sale as the 60 and 75 respectively.

The known prototypes are listed in the adjacent table, which has been compiled from references scattered throughout surviving Rover documents. The earliest mention of a P3 prototype found so far dates from early July 1947, when at the Board meeting of 4 July S. B. Wilks reported that works director Geoffrey Savage had taken a P3 to the continent for test purposes. It is not clear which one this was, but the most likely candidate is P3/P1.

On 23 July, John Toft-Bate, the industrial photographer who worked for Rover at the time, recorded in his notebook that he had photographed a 'P3 12hp Sports experimental model,' a description that suggests a four-light Sports Saloon, although at least some of the pictures in the set showed a six-light model. On 8 September, he photographed a cream 16hp model, and it may be one of these photographs that was used in *The Autocar* of 13 February 1948; it was registered as GAC 511, which identifies it as prototype P3/P3 (*see* the table of prototypes). GAC 511 also earned a mention in a notebook kept by chassis designer Gordon Bashford, although with no further comment except that it was a P3.

The P3 had a wider radiator grille than its predecessor, and its standard auxiliary lamp was mounted on a plinth ahead of this. GAC 915 was prototype P3/2/14 and had a 14hp IOE engine that was not put into production. Its grille badge also identifies it as a Rover 14.

ROVER P3 PROTOTYPES

At least two 'mule' prototypes were used to test various items that were eventually used for P3.

DDU 588	Registered in February 1938. Four-cylinder IOE engine and a prototype box-section frame under the body of a Ten saloon. Used by Maurice Wilks. By the time it was converted into the Rover Special single-seater racing car, it also had independent front suspension.
ENX 911	Probably registered in early 1945 (the ENX series began in September 1944), and known to have been taxed to 31 December 1945. Black six-light saloon with 16hp six-cylinder IOE engine (number SH/2/16/2). Used by S. B. Wilks.

Engine numbers appear to break down as follows:

SH/2/14/3	Sloping Head, second batch or type, 14hp, third engine
SH/2/16/2	Sloping Head, second batch or type, 16hp, second engine

(N.B. It is possible that the first batch or type were built before the war, and that the second batch or type were the post-war engines.)

Surviving records suggest that two groups of experimental cars were built before production began. The first group consisted of prototypes that were put on the road between approximately summer 1946 and October 1947. The second and smaller group appears to have been pilot-production cars that probably dated from late 1947 or very early 1948, although they were not road-registered until October 1949 and probably ran on trade plates before that.

Prototypes

No record of a P3/P2 has so far been found, and this list assumes that the two cars P3/2/14 and P3/2/16 took their position within the prototype group.

P3/P1	Registered EWD 584 and existed by mid-June 1946; the EWD numbers were first issued in May 1946. 12hp engine. Sold to Associated Aluminium Co, nr Coventry, in March 1953.
P3/2/14	Registered GAC 915 on 2 October 1947. 14hp engine, number SH/2/14/3. Sold to dealer Rosenfield of Manchester in June 1951.
P3/2/16	Registered GAC 916 on 2 October 1947. 16hp engine, number SH/2/16/4. Scrapped in the Service Department in October 1949.
P3/P3	Registered GAC 511 in approximately September 1947. Six-light saloon, probably cream with 16hp engine. Used by Rover's Peter Wilks from April 1951.
P3/P4	Registered GAC 980 on 3 October 1947. 16hp engine, number P3/P4; later re-engined with P4 75 engine number 0430-0465. Sold to dealer Gethins of Tyseley in January 1951.
P3/P5	Registered GNX 239 in approximately October 1947. Possibly the car described in Gordon Bashford's notebook as 'P3 no 5' and therefore a 14hp. Sold to dealer Rossleigh of Dundee in September 1949.

Pilot-Production Cars

There is some confusion about the identities of the two known cars. The record of cars despatched second-hand shows P3/2 as JNX 323 and P3/3 as JAC 464 but the record of company-owned vehicles shows the registration numbers the other way round. There may have been a P3/1 (and possibly others), but no records have so far been found.

P3/2	Registered JNX 323 on 3 October 1949. Rover 60, with engine number P3/2. Used by Rover Transport Department. Broken up (no date recorded).
P3/3	Registered JAC 464 on 3 October 1949. Rover 60, with engine number P3/3. Used by Rover Transport Department. Broken up (no date recorded).

Early Production

On 22 January 1948, S. B. Wilks told his colleagues on the Rover Board that production of the new P3 models had begun. He hoped that a few cars would be completed by early February, and at the Board's next meeting of 19 February he was able to report that the first cars had indeed been completed. The cars completed in February were all six-light Saloons, some with the four-cylinder engine and some with the six-cylinder type. The four-light types followed a little later: the first 75s were built in March but the 60s did not enter production until May.

As production got under way, two 75 six-light Saloons were earmarked as motor show cars. Rover's system of allocating chassis numbers to firm orders ensured that neither had a very early number, and also gives a good idea of how many orders must have been placed before production actually began.

Rover clearly believed that the maroon paint they had chosen for production suited the car well, and both the show cars had it. The car that introduced the new Rover to the world was L841-0144, which was shipped in early February to Rover's Belgian importer, Etablissements Paul Sterckx, and was shown on the Rover stand at the Brussels Autosalon that opened on 14 February. The next of the year's shows was at Geneva in March, and for that one the Rover exhibit was R841-0032, which had actually been completed more than three weeks after the Brussels car. The importer involved this time was Karl Vorster in Zurich, who was determined to make a splash and augmented the Rover exhibit with a Sports Saloon, L843-0043, specially finished by the factory in Duo Silver Grey with blue upholstery.

Rover's managing director S. B. Wilks attended the Geneva show himself, and told the Board meeting of 23 March that the cars had been well received. Nevertheless, he added, the body lines were subject to some criticism as being old-fashioned. This was an unsurprising comment, and Wilks had already reported at the February Board meeting that the P3's appearance was considered out of date by overseas buyers. As no cars had actually been sold by that date, he was probably quoting the opinions of Rover agents outside the UK who had seen the new cars or photographs of them in advance of their launch.

On the European continent, the show season continued with events in Amsterdam at the end of April and in Barcelona in May. The Land-Rover took pride of place at Amsterdam, although the show car was flanked by an unidentified example of the new P3 saloon, and then both were displayed at Barcelona. It must have been an attractive display: the 75 Sports Saloon (843-0023) and the Land-Rover were both finished in the same attractive light 'No 2' Green.

For the home show at London's Earl's Court that opened on 27 October, Rover clearly pulled out all the stops. Its own stand, number 161, had no fewer than four examples of the new model; Pressed Steel, who built the P3 bodyshells, had another one on stand 120; and coachbuilder Tickford on stand 126 had one of the two prototype 75 Drophead Coupés. On the Rover stand were a green 60 Sports Saloon, a grey 75 six-light Saloon, a 75 Sports Saloon and the second Drophead Coupé prototype, finished in maroon. They were kept company by one of the new Tickford-bodied Land-Rover station wagons; ordinary Land-Rovers were commercial vehicles and were not welcome at the motor show, but the station wagon was a passenger-carrier and merited a place. Pressed Steel showed a maroon 75 Sports Saloon, and the Drophead Coupé on the Tickford stand was probably finished in grey.

This would be the only London motor show where the P3 models would be displayed. By the time of the 1949 Show, the new P4 saloons would take centre stage on the Rover stand.

Early Press Reactions

Meanwhile, Rover had begun to prime the motoring press in Britain. The first result, which was

The radiator grille was surmounted by an enamelled metal badge in traditional Rover style, with the model type displayed on the sails of the Viking ship.

A similar badge was mounted on the boot lid, in the centre of the spare wheel pressing. The red reflectors were mounted differently on this car from the one pictured earlier.

more than a little discreet, was a report on IOE engine design that was published in *The Motor* for 28 January 1948. It was not directly associated with Rover, but there was a heavy hint in its reference to Jack Swaine's paper delivered to the Institution of Mechanical Engineers at Glasgow in November 1947. Full details of the P3 models were then released in early February, and with them came a new advertising slogan. The Rovers of the late 1930s and their revived siblings of 1946–1947 had been 'One of Britain's Fine Cars'; the new 60 and 75 now became 'One of Britain's Fine Cars – Now Made Finer!'

'This very fine new model is a great credit to its makers,' said *The Autocar* of 13 February 1948, 'and is likely still further to add to their specialist's reputation.' The new engines delivered 'not only a considerable improvement in performance but at the same time a reduction in fuel consumption, which is a remarkable double achievement in engineering.' *The Motor* of 18 February meanwhile praised the 'really advanced design practice' of the engine and chassis. *The Motor World* of 13 February noted that 'the coachwork follows previous lines but with a number of improvements,' while 'the chassis throughout has been completely redesigned.' Specialist publication *Automobile Engineer* also published a very thorough eleven-page examination of the chassis and engines in its July 1948 issue – although it passed

A TRIPLE-CARBURETTOR 75

Quite late in the 1949 season, Rover fitted a 75 four-light saloon (registered HWD 206) with a three-carburettor installation. This car still survives in enthusiast hands. It was probably built to test the three-carburettor configuration as part of the development programme for the P4 75, which, as a heavier car than the P3, needed a more powerful version of the six-cylinder engine to maintain performance standards. A former owner of the car believes that six such cars were built, all from four-light models.

However, both Jack Swaine and Maurice Wilks were opposed to multiple-carburettor installations, arguing that they were difficult to maintain. Now that Rover was exporting cars to overseas markets where little mechanical expertise might be available, multiple carburettors were a hostage to fortune. In the end, the P4 75 entered production with just two carburettors – and Rover went to a single-carburettor engine with a larger swept volume as soon as they could.

This 1949 four-light 75 is one that was fitted with a triple-carburettor installation as part of the P4 development programme. It is finished in No 2 Green, the colour that was also used on the contemporary Land-Rover, and it has one of the optional-extra Viking's head mascots mounted on its radiator filler cap.

no comment on the bodies, beyond acknowledging that there were two different types.

On Sale

Such enthusiasm in the motoring press was all very well, but restrictions on new car sales in Britain meant that only the privileged few could actually get their hands on a P3. In practice, the first 75 (number 841-0001) was not despatched-out until 2 March, when it went to Henlys, Rover's main London distributor.

By this time, Rover had two years' experience of the export market and of the government's insistence on giving priority to overseas sales. There were many overseas dealerships in place that were ready to take the new cars as soon as they became available, and for the first time the company had also established arrangements for overseas assembly in a limited number of countries as well.

So P3 production was geared to export from the beginning, although at that Board meeting on 19 February S. B. Wilks was able to tell his

PRICES FOR THE P3 ROVERS, 1948–1949

Six-light and four-light models had the same showroom prices.

		Retail price	Purchase tax	Total
1948	60	£845 0s 0d	£235 9s 6d	£1,080 9s 6d
	75	£865 0s 0d	£241 0s 7d	£1,106 0s 7d
1949	60	The 1949 models appear to have had the same prices as the 1948 ones		
	75			

The 75 Drophead Coupé was announced in October 1948 with a price of £1,277 5s 0d (£999 retail plus £278 5s 0d purchase tax).

Exports remained important during the P3 years, and these cars are seen in the showroom of Annand & Thompson, the Australian distributor based in Brisbane. In the background are examples of the 1947 models. Rovers were very popular in Australia and there was a two-year waiting list for a new one.

fellow directors that the Ministry of Supply had agreed to relax its export requirement to ease the changeover to the new models, and that the first 150 to 200 cars could be sold on the home market. This early experience would give Rover a chance to make any minor corrections needed before they began to export the cars in quantity.

The Solihull assembly lines turned out both RHD and LHD examples for export, and most P3s were in fact sold overseas after a slow start. S. B. Wilks told the Rover Board on 26 April 1948 that the proportion of cars exported had not reached its target during the first quarter of the year, but that the Ministry of Supply understood this was due to the changeover of models. For June, Rover were aiming to export 60 per cent of production, and the figure gradually improved. In May 1949, for example, the Rover Board heard that 70 per cent of that month's car production had been exported. (The proportion of Land-Rovers was even greater, at 85 per cent.)

Rover was still learning how to deal with exports most effectively, and as the European continent was a major sales target, the early sales brochure was printed in French and Dutch as well as in English; there may have been versions in other languages, too. Many sales were made in British colonies, where there was a more or less captive audience, and delays in shipping led to an interesting situation in Australia, where the new 75 was promoted in a sales brochure alongside the last of the old Twelves and Sixteens during 1948.

It was Rover practice at the time to number cars with LHD and RHD within the same sequence. Export models had an L or an R prefix to indicate their steering position, and cars intended for the home market had no letter prefix. However, the position was not quite as simple as that makes it sound. Surviving records make very clear that Rover built far more cars for RHD export markets than ever found buyers abroad, and there were very many cases of cars with an R-prefix identification going straight to Rover dealers in the UK. This might have been a deliberate policy: it made good sense to build cars suitable for export that could be shipped immediately if orders arrived. On the other hand, if orders came in from the UK and there were no overseas orders to be met, it was better to sell these cars than to stockpile them in the hope of future orders.

As the table of production figures at the end of this chapter shows, the twenty months of P3 production were divided into two 'seasons' or model-years of unequal length. The 1948 season was eleven months long (February to December) while the 1949 season lasted for only nine months (January to September). Even so, more than twice as many P3s were built in the first season as in the second, which rather suggests that the model's appeal had already started to wane.

The last P3 models were actually built at Solihull in September 1949, and there is no record of any ceremony, formal or informal, to commemorate the occasion. As for the four-light 60 models, which were always the slowest-selling models, their production had already come to an end some five months earlier, in April.

Despite their short production run and 'stopgap' design, the P3 models seem to have been very much liked. They certainly earned the approval of the Wiltshire Police, who bought a number for patrol duties. The enthusiasm of the motoring press remained undimmed, too. *The Autocar* did not carry out a full road test until its issue of 4 February 1949, but was then just as full of praise as it had been in its initial assessment a year earlier. The test car was a 75 registered HAC 891, which the magazine described as:

...no ordinary car.... By scrupulous attention to things that matter beneath as well as on the surface, Rover's have succeeded in providing a very special refinement of running, as well as a host of carefully studied features, both mechanical and in the bodywork fittings, that mean more in comfort and safety and convenience of the user than words can easily describe.

Rover were so pleased with that report that they were quoting extracts from it in advertising for the 75 a month later. The extract ran:

Briefly this thoroughly satisfying car of the highest quality does everything with a silky smoothness, a soothing quietness, and also in about the highest degree of riding comfort in front and back seats yet known, and with a precision and lightness of control which makes the driver feel on top of his form and which renders every mile a delight whether in town or out on the open road... Throughout, there is that suggestion of top mechanical quality, exclusive to a tiny fraction of cars, which eludes detailed description.

By that autumn, when the P4 was just about to be announced as the P3's replacement, *The Autocar* was still enthusing about it. One of its staff took HAC 891 on a two-day trip to Wales, and came back deeply impressed.

I suggest,

he wrote in the issue of 4 September 1949,

...that a Rover 75 is stowed away in an attic, so that if it be centuries hence when the instinct towards craftsmanship returns to this country, and car manufacturers are seeking for a Chippendale piece to inspire them, they can go to the attic, unwrap the 75 and say, 'Look, this is how they built them in the great days of British car making'.

Production Changes

Rover made as few changes as possible to the P3s, not least because they were always intended as short-term products. This probably explains why the Provisional Workshop Manual (publication number TP/107/A) that was ready by January 1948 was never updated or even turned into a definitive publication: there was simply no need.

However, there were changes to the engines. Only the first 430 four-cylinder engines (and two later examples) had the original high-compression (7.36:1) pistons, and after that they switched to the low-compression pistons (7.05:1) used in the Land-Rover. This change was probably due to nothing more sinister than manufacturing economy. The six-cylinder engines also switched to low-compression pistons after 3,020 examples had been made, the compression ratio dropping from 7.52:1 down to 7.25:1.

A change was also made to the front suspension quite late in the production run. It appears that the original IFS gave poor control of small

COLOURS AND TRIMS, ROVER P3 60 AND 75 MODELS

The same five colours and combinations were used in both the 1948 and the 1949 seasons. These combinations were identified by numbers, as shown in the table below.

Wings and bodies were always the same colour, and there were no standard two-tone colour schemes, Wheels were painted to match the bodywork, and all radiator stoneguards were enamelled in silver. All woodwork was polished walnut, and leather upholstery was standard. The single coachline ('fine line') on each side was hand-painted.

Only seven combinations were listed in the salesman's manual in March 1948. Three others were introduced during production (nos 8–10); these are unidentified, although no 8 was probably Black with Grey upholstery and no 10 had Grey as the main colour. No1 Sundown was not generally available but a small batch was done in approximately June 1948. There were also a few special-order cars, with colours that included Black with Grey, Grey with Green, and Duo Grey.

	Body colour	Fine lines	Upholstery	Headlining
No1	Sundown	Dark Maroon	Brown	Fawn
No2	Green	Dark Green	Green	Green
No3	Grey	Blue	Blue	Blue-grey
No4	Maroon	Gold	Maroon	Fawn
No5	Black	Gold	Brown	Fawn
No6	Black	Green	Green	Green
No7	Black	Maroon	Maroon	Fawn

The 'No2 Green' combination was also used for the first Land-Rovers, although with leathercloth rather than leather upholstery.

Few pictures of the Tickford dropheads exist. This shows the Tickford stand at the 1948 motor show, with a dark (probably grey) car alongside the then-new Land-Rover station wagon, which was also bodied by Tickford.

wheel movements, and engineer George Mackie remembered driving a car with the front wing removed so that he could watch the suspension in action to determine what was happening. The problem was narrowed down to the Armstrong lever-arm dampers, and so the system was redesigned to use a new top wishbone and telescopic dampers. The revised suspension was introduced at cars numbered 921-0750, 923-0325, 941-4030 and 943-2027, probably some time around January 1949. Service literature also shows that a conversion kit was available to update earlier cars, although there are no records to suggest how many cars were actually modified.

Lastly, there was a minor change to the brass centre caps of the hubcaps. A new mould was clearly introduced at some point in production, bringing with it minor differences in the finished product, but it is not clear when this occurred.

Of some interest is that in the early 1950s, Rover fitted the twin-carburettor P4 version of the 2103cc six-cylinder cars into a number of customers' P3s, both 75s and 60s, presumably mainly to give better performance.

The Drophead Coupés

There are still some uncertainties about the story of the Drophead Coupés, although it is beyond doubt that Rover hoped to get them into production alongside the four-light and six-light Saloons, even though the P3 range was always destined for a relatively short production life.

At least two were built, and possibly three. According to Dennis C. Mynard (in *Salmons & Sons, the Tickford Coachbuilders*), during 1948 Rover supplied Tickford with a 75 chassis 'with a saloon body, less doors, boot lid and rear seat, for conversion into a drophead coupé'. Rover records suggest that this was a six-light model, 841-0406, which dated from mid-March, although the finished car was given a new chassis number.

Tickford body designer Winston Chater drew up a three-position drophead similar to the pre-war Rover style. There was a little more to the conversion than beheading the saloon body, because the P3's 'three-quarters' chassis needed some additional strengthening at the rear. A team of body builders under Tickford's Dick Croot nevertheless 'removed the roof and rear body panels' and rebuilt the body using 'composite framing of best ash and plywood.'

This first car was followed by a second, but in this case there is no indication that Tickford received a complete car. Quite probably, they requested a chassis, powertrain and front-end panels, and simply created the rest themselves. This second car must have been built up in the spring or early summer, and probably had no important differences from the first one. The two cars were then numbered in a dedicated chassis sequence as 844-0001 and 844-0002.

Both were displayed at the Earl's Court motor show in October 1948, one on the Rover stand and one on the Tickford stand. The Rover car was painted maroon and had a grey convertible top and matching leather upholstery. The Tickford example was probably grey, although that has not been confirmed. Confusingly, both were recorded by the Rover despatch department as being grey. Rover were certainly serious about putting the model on sale: the show catalogue listed its price as £1,277 5s 0d (which broke down as £999 plus £278 5s 0d purchase tax), and had prepared a single-sheet flyer to promote it. It must be said this was perhaps not their best effort, with an artist's impression of the car rather than an actual photograph.

The Rover 75 Tickford Drophead Foursome Coupé, as it was called, attracted surprisingly little comment in the press, although *The Autocar* did picture the car on the Tickford stand in its show review of 5 November 1948. Both cars were sent to the Rover factory after the motor show ended on Saturday 6 November, where they were logged in to the despatch department on Monday 15 November; it is likely that they had spent part of the intervening period at Rover's London service depot in Seagrave Road. And then everything went horribly quiet.

There may have been more than one reason for the demise of the drophead coupé project. First, over the summer of 1948 Rover had asked Tickford to undertake volume construction of the special body for the Land-Rover station wagon, and in view of the shortages of raw material that were then affecting the motor industry, something probably had to give. The Land-Rover looked like being a greater money-spinner than the drophead P3, and so took priority. Second, Rover was simply extremely busy in the second half of 1948, scrambling to meet high demand for the Land-Rover while trying to get the P4 ready for production the following summer. In the face of all this, the P3 drophead project simply lapsed, and on 9 June 1949 the two prototype cars went to the Gethin's dealership at Tyseley for onward sale to the public.

There is one further drophead P3 mystery. The undated entry in the despatch department record for car number 941-3457 in approximately March 1949 reads 'Drophead Coupé' but gives no further details. This is clearly far too late to have been the car that provided elements of the second Tickford prototype in summer 1948, but no further traces of it have been found.

THE GRABER P3

The Tickford cars apart, just one P3 chassis was supplied to a coachbuilder for special bodywork. This was chassis number R843-1157, drawn from the 75 four-light sequence, which was given a body by the Swiss coachbuilder Carrosserie Graber.

Graber was one of the great Swiss coachbuilders, who gained fame during the 1930s as a builder of mainly cabriolet bodies. After World War II, he focused his attention largely on British-built chassis, but this was the only Rover he bodied in the 1940s, and was also his earliest known work on a Rover chassis. (He would go on to work on Rover P5 and P6 models in the 1960s, and possibly also constructed a P4 convertible in the 1950s.)

According to the Rover despatch records, this 75 left Solihull in 'chassis-only' form on 15 September 1948. It was shipped to the Swiss Rover agents Baumberger und Vorster in Zurich, whose Karl Vorster sent it to Graber at Wichtrach to be bodied as a two-door cabriolet for his own use. Graber's ledger records it as body number 602 alongside a date of 25 October 1948, which is likely to have been the completion date.

The cabriolet body was made of steel, and Graber had to extend the chassis to support its rear end. The design was remarkably sleek and modern in appearance, although it retained the traditional upright Rover grille and had clearly-defined wing outlines as well. The car was finished in off-white with a tan hood in Graber's characteristic style, with neither side windows behind the doors nor the external hood irons favoured by German coachbuilders.

The Graber 75 appeared on the coachbuilder's stand at the 1949 Geneva motor show, and *The Autocar* for March 25 that year described it as 'one of the show highlights'. In 1953, it was sold to a Briton working at the NATO headquarters in Paris. It came to Britain in 1962 after being sold to one of this man's colleagues, and had no fewer than eight more owners before it was given a comprehensive restoration in 2003. It is now regularly seen at Rover club events.

Swiss coachbuilder Graber took a totally different approach to building a drophead coupé. This picture shows the car when new...

... and this is how it survives today.

Rover did not give up on the idea on a drophead model altogether; they simply switched their attention to their newer chassis and asked Tickford to draw up a drophead coupé body to suit that instead. As for the later history of the Tickford-bodied P3 cars, there is again a lack of information. The last known trace of the maroon show car is an advertisement on page 62 of *The Autocar* dated 29 June 1956, when it was for sale at £495 by a dealer in London's Kensington district.

CKD: The Overseas Assembly Operations

Rover had no tradition of overseas assembly in the late 1940s, although the company did briefly operate a factory in New Zealand in 1930–1931 that closed down when exchange rates became unfavourable. Nevertheless, overseas assembly was an attractive option at a time when exports were of such vital importance to the company's future. There are no clear references to any plans in the surviving records of the Rover Board, but the company must have planned for overseas assembly of the P3 saloons from an early stage in their development, because the earliest shipments of cars to overseas assembly plants were made in March 1948, shortly after production had begun at Solihull. The cars pioneered the system; the much more widely known exports of Land-Rovers for overseas assembly did not begin until August 1949, some seventeen months later.

Overseas assembly operations of this type are often known as CKD operations. Those letters standard for 'Completely Knocked Down', which is a description of the kits of parts that are shipped abroad, and Rover's own internal documentation refers to CKD 'sets'. One 'set' built one car, and in practice Rover always shipped its cars (and Land-Rovers) in batches of six, supposedly because this made the most cost-effective use of the space available.

Rover established CKD operations in just three countries for the P3 models, and these were probably used at least partly for familiarisation with the system so that it could later be expanded and most efficiently exploited for overseas Land-Rover assembly. The three countries were India, where the operation was run by Dewars Garage in Calcutta; Eire, where the operation was run by Lincoln & Nolan in Dublin; and New Zealand, where the operation was shared by several dealerships but its actual location remains unknown.

To Rover, the value of its CKD operations was that they increased the percentage of its products that could be exported. Some overseas countries imposed high import taxes on vehicles brought in from overseas, but encouraged in-territory assembly of vehicles because this provided work for the local labour force. The regulations were complex, differed from one country to the next, and were liable to change from one year to the next as well. There were also differences between one country and the next as a result of differences in the skills available within the local workforce, and the local availability or otherwise of such items as tyres, glass, batteries and paint.

The description 'CKD' tended to be used rather loosely for many years, and in its strictest sense describes assembly from a completely disassembled state. The Rover operations involving the P3 models did not go this far; they appear to have been what is now more generally described as SKD ('Semi-Knocked Down') types, in which the vehicles are shipped as major assemblies. Some are even described in the despatch department records as 'P/B', which presumably stands for 'Part Built'. It is also clear from the despatch records that the Indian operation took bodies that had already been painted at Solihull; the Dublin operation began with pre-painted bodies but from December 1948 took bodies finished in primer and painted them itself; and the first two bodies for the New Zealand operation were painted black, but the later ones appear to have been unpainted. The records show that the final cars for Dublin from May 1949 were provided with upholstery in maroon, although it may be that this was the only occasion when the upholstery colour was recorded.

A total of 390 P3 models were assembled from CKD in 1948–1949. The largest quantity was built in India; Eire lagged a long way behind; and the New Zealand operation was short-lived. There was no overseas assembly of the four-light models, although the 75 four-light chassis shipped to Switzerland to be bodied as a cabriolet by Graber is described in the despatch records as 'CKD'.

The breakdown is as follows:

Dewars Garage, Calcutta		(282 cars)
60 six-light	April 1948 to March 1949	66
75 six-light	March 1948 to March 1949	216
Lincoln & Nolan, Dublin		(72 cars)
60 six-light	October 1948 to June 1949	30
75 six-light	May 1948 to July 1949	42
New Zealand		(36 cars)
75 six-light	April to May 1949	36

The New Zealand cars were shared around dealers as follows: Broadway Parking (6), Christchurch Car Exchange (6), Khyber Pass Motors (12) and Wellington Motors (12).

CHASSIS NUMBERS AND PRODUCTION TOTALS, ROVER P3 60 AND 75 MODELS

The chassis numbers of cars destined for export were prefixed by R (for RHD) or L (for LHD) as appropriate. Home-market cars had no prefix letter. The CKD models were numbered in the standard sequences.

Note that a dash is used here between the identifying type prefix and the serial number to aid clarity; it does not appear on the chassis plates themselves.

Chassis numbers and engine numbers did not normally match, although a few early ones did (841-0001, for example, did have engine number 841-0001). Engines were numbered in two sequences – 821 for the four-cylinder and 841 for the six-cylinder. The 821 engines were used in both 1948 and 1949 60s, and the 841 engines in both 1948 and 1949 75s.

Season	*Type*	*Chassis sequence*	*Total*
1948	60 Saloon (six-light)	821-0001 to 821-0655	655
	60 four-light	823-0001 to 823-0304	304
	75 Saloon (six-light)	841-0001 to 841-3441	3,441
	75 four-light	843-0001 to 843-1721	1,721
	75 Drophead Coupé	844-0001 to 844-0002	2
1949	60 Saloon (six-light)	921-0656 to 921-0911	256
	60 four-light	923-0305 to 923-0363	59
	75 Saloon (six-light)	941-3442 to 941-5196	1,755
	75 four-light	943-1722 to 943-2640	919

Notes:
One 841-series 75 Saloon (841-0406) appears to have been converted into one of the Tickford Drophead Coupé prototypes.
One 843-series 75 four-light (R843-1157) was delivered in chassis-only form and was bodied by Graber.
One 941-series 75 Saloon (941-3457) appears to have been converted to a Drophead Coupé.

	1948	**1949**	**Total**
60	959	315	1,274
75	5,164	2,674	7,838
Total	6,123	2,989	**9,112**

CHAPTER 6

Experimentation: Gas Turbines

Rover's involvement with research into gas turbine engines began by chance during the early years of World War II. In 1940, the air ministry selected the company to help Frank Whittle get his promising jet aircraft engine designs into production, and the intention was that Rover should handle the production as well. For three years, a group of Rover engineers, led by Maurice Wilks, worked on the Whittle jet and made some major contributions to its design. However, Whittle was not happy at having his ideas altered by others, despite the brief from the air ministry, and friction developed between him and the Rover engineers. Realising that this friction could not be allowed to endanger what they saw as a vital project, the air ministry brokered a deal between Rover and Rolls-Royce in 1943. Rover surrendered its jet engine work to Rolls-Royce, and in return took over work on the Meteor tank engine.

Pioneering Development

Those three years of work had clearly piqued Maurice Wilks' interest. Always enthusiastic about new engineering possibilities, he had begun to wonder about how the jet engine could be adapted to suit cars. There was no question of using it in the same way as in aircraft, of course – the hot exhaust gases that provided forward thrust in the air would be simply dangerous on the ground. However, those gases could be converted into rotary motion by passing them across a turbine wheel. This could then be connected very simply to drive the wheels of a car. As the 'jet' of gases was not the sole driving force in such an engine, it was re-named a gas turbine. And by 1945, Maurice Wilks was determined that Rover should look at developing it for road cars.

Wilks was not alone in recognising the potential of the gas turbine engine, and he discussed his thoughts with Henry Spurrier at Leyland. Leyland agreed to take a financial stake in the gas turbine experiments, but chose to leave the development work to Rover. So, by the end of 1945, Wilks had the agreements he wanted and was preparing to establish a gas turbines research team at Rover's new factory in Solihull.

Project Department C was established at the beginning of 1946, its rather odd name helping to conceal the nature of its activities. Whether there was a real need for such secrecy is not clear, but perhaps Wilks saw the gas turbine research as pioneering work that needed to be concealed from other motor manufacturers. He and other

Few pictures were taken inside Project Department C, but this one shows one of the test beds for the gas turbine engines. It was probably taken in 1946.

Rover people had come into close contact with military secrecy and its practices during the war years, and the name of the new department certainly seemed to reflect that. There was even a believable cover story associated with it, that the department was working on diesel engines and on sleeve-valve types. Needless to say, no evidence of any such work actually being done has ever come to light.

The new department had a minimal budget in the beginning, and it only had two employees. Both had been recruited from Rolls-Royce. One was Frank Bell, a New Zealander and aero engine expert. The other was Spen King, a nephew of the Wilks brothers who had just finished his apprenticeship. It was their job to scale down jet engine technology to a size suitable for a motor car, and to harness the output of such an engine to drive that car's rear wheels.

Gas Turbine Prototypes

It took about a year before the first prototype gas turbine engine was running. On the way, there had been some failures and the occasional exploding engine. In an engine that was physically smaller than an aircraft jet engine, reducing the size of everything proportionately also led to reduced efficiency. Another problem was that cost and availability issues meant that some of the exotic materials used in the aero engines would be impractical in an engine for a road vehicle. Bell and King were aiming for an output of about 150bhp, but their first successful engine, called T5, actually delivered just 100bhp.

If 100bhp does not sound a great deal by modern standards, in 1947 it was impressive. For perspective, it is worth remembering that the 2.1-litre petrol engine in Rover's forthcoming

Rover's first working gas turbine engine was the T5, which produced 100bhp. It first ran in 1947 and was displayed in public in 1948, breaking the secrecy around the work of Project Department C.

P3 75 saloon had just 72bhp, and that the T5 gas turbine was around 200lb lighter in weight than a four-cylinder P4 60 engine that promised just 60bhp. Against such a background, it is not difficult to see why Rover's engineers saw such potential for the gas turbine engine.

The T5 engine first ran on 3 February 1947, but Rover continued to treat their gas turbine research as secret. Among the ideas they continued to pursue was that of using the waste heat in the exhaust gases to warm the incoming air and so improve combustion, but at that time no heat-exchangers of a suitable size were available. Work based on the T5 engine was still in progress just over a year later, when Rover were provoked into revealing something of their work by publicity surrounding another company's efforts with gas turbine engines.

Centrax Power Units had been founded in 1946 at Acton in London by Richard Barr and Geoffrey White, both former members of Frank Whittle's jet engine team. They displayed a small gas turbine engine at the 1948 British Industries Fair in Birmingham and claimed it could be used in a car. Rover reacted by contacting *Autocar* magazine and offering the story of their own work, which was published in the magazine's issues of 7 and 14 May 1948. They did not specifically claim that their gas turbine engine could be used in a car, but allowed *Autocar* editor Geoffrey Smith to make the suggestion. The cat was now pretty much out of the bag.

Further Development

The next significant step followed in 1949, when the Rover team moved on to working on a further developed and more powerful engine called T8. A pair of engines were put into *Torquil*, a former wartime torpedo recovery boat that S. B. Wilks owned, for evaluation. Of interest is that Tony Poole, then a fitter on the gas turbine team, remembered driving with a colleague from Solihull to Anglesey, where Wilks kept his boat, 'on a gas turbine job'. The car they used was one of the two Studebakers that Rover had bought to study in connection with the design of the forthcoming Rover P4 saloon (*see* Chapter 8).

The two T8 engines in *Torquil* acquitted themselves well, and gave the gas turbines team enough confidence to move onto the next stage – which was to attempt a car installation. They enlisted the help of Rover's chief chassis designer, Gordon Bashford, to draw up an appropriate installation, and it was more or less inevitable that a Rover 75 – in its latest P4 guise – should be chosen as the host car.

There was much more to this than hauling the six-cylinder engine out of the 75 and dropping a gas turbine engine into its place. The biggest problem was that a gas turbine engine produces a very large volume of hot exhaust gases, and that some way of ensuring these emerged behind the car was necessary. Bashford's solution was to mount the engine amidships, more or less where the back seat of the saloon would normally be. The exhaust then had a relatively short run through large ducts that emerged through the panels just above and behind the engine.

This arrangement had two consequences. One was that the car would only have room for three occupants on a bench seat in the front, and the other was that retaining its saloon body was no longer feasible. So the body was drawn up as an open type, with a large fixed windscreen. To get the standard saloon body turned into what they wanted, Rover handed the car over to Salmons-Tickford at Newport Pagnell. Tickfords had built the pre-war Rover drophead coupés and during 1948 the prototypes of the P3 drophead cars as well, and were also committed to building the bodies for the Land-Rover station wagon of the time, so they were an obvious choice. They made an excellent job of the gas turbine car, retaining the lines of the saloon's lower body but turning it into a sleek-looking two-door. For good measure, it was painted in a pearlescent greenish-grey colour, not unlike a modern metallic paint but in 1949 very much cutting-edge technology.

Although the gas turbine car was in effect converted from a P4 75 saloon, in practice Rover seem not to have used a complete car but to have taken a rolling chassis and some body panels and built the car up around its gas turbine engine. Rover knew by now that this could produce as much as 230bhp at full stretch, but in the interests of durability decided to limit it to a distinctly conservative 100bhp in the car. The T8 engine was installed with its drive pinion towards the front of the car, and this was geared to a large-diameter reduction gear with a step-down ratio

Gas turbine car XT1 as first built, with a tall fixed windscreen. The picture was probably taken during early test runs at a local airfield. From left to right behind the car are Maurice Wilks, S. B. Wilks and Frank Bell.

In the beginning, the gas turbine car was transported in a covered trailer towed behind an 80-inch Land-Rover that had been specially converted with a fifth wheel.

of 7.55:1. This in turn drove a transfer gear alongside that turned the drive through 180 degrees and took it to the rear axle by a propellor shaft running beside the engine. The final drive, offset from the centre line of the axle as in the standard saloon, had a nearly conventional 3.64:1 ratio.

Versatile Performance

There was no need for a gearbox with a range of ratios because, rather like an electric motor, the gas turbine engine generated enough low-speed torque for starting from rest and had a wide enough rev range to allow any reasonable speed – and more, as it would turn out later. Nor was there any need for a clutch; when the car was idling, it was simply prevented from moving by applying the brakes, in much the same way as on a modern automatic. Nevertheless, Rover did add a reverse gear in the driveline, behind the transfer gear, to allow the car to be manoeuvred more easily.

The gas turbine car never had a standard P4 chassis number, but it must have had one of the first 250 or so chassis that were built. It nevertheless needed some kind of identity number and was given the prototype designation XT1 (eXperimental Turbine car no 1). Spen King did not remember anyone ever calling it that, though, and to the members of the gas turbine team it was simply the Turbine Car.

From start to finish, the Turbine Car took six weeks to build. Its engine was installed on Friday, 3 March 1950, and an excited gas turbines team took it for its first test runs the very next day to an airfield near Solihull. This has not been firmly identified but is likely to have been Wellesbourne, near Stratford-on-Avon. The only problem of any significance that showed up was caused by the windscreen, which created eddies that sucked the exhaust gases back into the passenger compartment. So the gas turbines team replaced it with a pair of aero screens that gave the car an even more sporting and purposeful look.

Both S. B. Wilks and Maurice Wilks were present at those first runs, and it was probably S. B. Wilks who decided to capitalise on the company's achievement without delay by demonstrating the car to the RAC's technical committee. A date was set for the following Thursday, 9 March, at the Silverstone race track.

However, inaccurate stories about the planned event appeared in some daily newspapers, and so the demonstration to the RAC officials was rearranged for Wednesday 8 March at the then-new MIRA proving ground. The Silverstone event nevertheless went ahead on the Thursday and was turned into a demonstration for the press – which turned out to be a good move because of the high level of interest shown in the car.

At MIRA in front of the RAC observers, the Turbine Car did five laps of the $2\frac{3}{4}$-mile perimeter track, once reaching nearly 90mph (145km/h). However, 'no attempt was made to attain maximum speed,' as the RAC's subsequent report noted, although 'in a test of acceleration from standstill, the car smoothly attained 60mph in 14 seconds.' That was impressively fast for a period when many family cars could barely reach 60mph, and when a powerful six-cylinder

There is no known colour photography from the first press event, but this picture has been colorised by Neil Castle to excellent effect. Maurice Wilks is in the driving seat, with Frank Bell next to him. By this time, twin aero screens had been fitted.

A gas turbine engine produces a large volume of exhaust gas, as Maurice Wilks demonstrated to a probably somewhat startled journalist.

car like the standard Rover 75 needed around 22 seconds to reach such a speed from rest.

The next day's runs in front of the press at Silverstone generated a huge amount of excitement and a huge amount of publicity for Rover, who capitalised on the car's success for some time afterwards in advertisements for their standard 75 saloon. As for the Centrax gas turbine engine, it had by this time disappeared from view, and never was put into a car to prove the claims made for it in 1948.

Building on this success, Rover displayed a 200bhp gas turbine engine at the Geneva motor show later that month, and then in April the Turbine Car was shipped to New York for that city's annual motor show, where it attracted considerable interest. Meanwhile, Rover were doing their best to make it road-legal. The licensing authorities had no policy for dealing with a car designed to run on paraffin, and it was not until somebody pointed out that the T8 engine could also run on petrol that the problem was resolved. In the meantime, Rover had managed to persuade the Rotherham licensing authority to issue the highly appropriate number JET 1 in advance; the rest of the JET series were not issued until March 1953! The Turbine Car became JET 1 on 13 May 1950, and has been known by that name ever since.

Industry Recognition

This period of the car's existence came to an end in January 1951, when the RAC presented the Dewar Trophy to the Rover company in recognition of its pioneering achievement. This was a

Road-registered as JET 1 over the summer of 1950, the car had also acquired a small union flag symbol on either side of its bonnet.

major accolade. Unlike some modern awards, which are presented annually to the most deserving effort in their respective fields, the Dewar award was only presented when something truly outstanding appeared. The last time it had been presented was in 1929, 21 years earlier.

Further development of the engine improved reliability, especially that of the turbine blades, until the gas turbine team were confident that the T8 could safely be run at its full 230bhp output. Further tests at MIRA showed that JET 1 was capable of 120mph (193km/h), and only the limitations of the track prevented it from exceeding that speed. Stopping it from high speeds was another matter altogether, though, and Spen King remembered running the car during earlier development when its T8 engine was rated at around 150–160bhp. With the original P4 saloon drum brakes, 'you had to be pretty careful!'.

Rover therefore approached Dunlop, who were then experimenting with disc brakes, and secured their co-operation in fitting discs on all four wheels of JET 1. This was a remarkably advanced development for 1952, and it allowed the project to move onto its next stage, which was some timed runs to establish speed records for a gas turbine-powered car.

The idea of the speed runs actually came from motoring journalist Montagu Tombs of *The Autocar*. Tombs was a great friend of Maurice Wilks, and the two used to go pistol-shooting together. Wilks knew how much good publicity Jaguar had gained from some officially-timed speed runs done with the XK120 sports car on the Jabbeke highway in Belgium in May 1949, and could see the potential benefit to Rover. So he instructed the gas turbine team to prepare JET 1 for some similar runs.

Spen King's first concern was to shed some weight from JET 1. He had its double-skinned rear bulkhead replaced by a single-skinned type and removed everything that was not necessary for the runs. That included the hubcaps (which would have flown off at speed, anyway) and even

Spen King did a great deal of work on the car to reduce weight, and a new front end reduced aerodynamic drag. Here he is at the wheel during the 1952 speed runs at Jabbeke, with Peter Wilks standing beside the car.

the jacking points. The bumpers went, too, and the original Cyclops nose was replaced by a much more streamlined design, which King himself drew up. Although generally similar to the latest, 1952-season P4 front end, it was actually quite different in detail. The new wings were made by Abbey Panels in Coventry, who had built the final Marauders (*see* Appendix IV). 'I took a lot of weight out of the car,' remembered King. 'It was something like 600lb! It made a big difference. The first time I drove it after that, it was just a completely different car. You could really feel it.'

The positions of the air inlets were also changed, mainly because they tended to suck in rubber shed by the tyres when the car was running at high speed. The exhaust outlets were relocated, partly to obtain neater and lighter ducting and partly to incorporate a certain amount of silencing. As there was no clutch, there was a real risk that the rear wheels would lock up at high speed if the engine failed, and so the reverse gear was removed and replaced by a freewheel. The original 7.55:1 step-down gearing was also changed for a 4.875:1 ratio to give higher top speeds at some cost to acceleration. The aero screens were removed and a detachable panel was made up to cover the passenger seat, while the driver was to be protected from the elements by a detachable streamlined 'blister' made of perspex. On test, however, this was found to mist up badly and so was never seen in public.

Trial Runs in Belgium

Following the Jaguar example in 1949, Rover decided to stage their speed runs at the Jabbeke highway in Belgium. This was the first stretch of the Ostend to Brussels motorway to be completed, and included a section that was straight, flat and several miles long. The Belgian authorities were happy for it to be used for high-speed testing, and the gendarmerie would oblige by closing down one carriageway. Meanwhile, the Royal Automobile Club of Belgium were happy to time runs and officiate generally. Well aware that Peter Wilks' Marauder venture was running into the sand, Rover management decided to help him out by paying him a fee to organise the record runs for JET 1. He booked two days' use of the Jabbeke highway for June 1952.

JET 1 was fitted with Dunlop road-racing tyres and the Rover gas turbine team took it to Belgium. Agreement was reached that Peter Wilks would do all the timed standing-start acceleration runs, and that Spen King would do the 'flying' distance runs. The runs began at 9am on the morning of Wednesday, 25 June, and King established average speeds of 140.422mph (225.987km/h) for the flying kilometre and 137.403mph (221.128km/h) for the flying mile – a tremendously impressive achievement right from the start. 'I remember it seemed quite a narrow two-lane motorway at that speed!' he admitted.

An air leak on the inlet side of the car's oil pump delayed the standing-start runs until 3.40pm when, with Peter Wilks at the wheel, JET 1 achieved a mean kilometre standing start speed of 82.391mph (132.595km/h) and a mean mile standing start speed of 95.568mph (153.801km/h). The Rover team decided to call a halt to the proceedings at that point, and to discuss the next stage. Their first day's work had after all achieved an historic double: the first time a car propelled by a non-reciprocating internal-combustion engine had been officially timed, and the first time kerosene had been used as a fuel when establishing road records.

That evening, JET 1's axle ratio was raised from 3.64:1 to 3.275:1, and the compressor was re-governed from 38,000rpm to 40,000rpm. At 8am the next morning, Spen King took the wheel of JET 1, and in cool, still air he achieved mean speeds of 151.965mph (245.563km/h) for the flying kilometre and 151.196mph (243.326km/h) for the flying mile. The car's maximum speed during these runs was in fact 152.691mph (245.732km/h), and King was convinced that more would have been possible if there had been a longer stretch of road available. 'It was still accelerating at those speeds,' he remembered.

Triumphant Return

The team returned jubilantly to Solihull, and Rover top management responded in typical fashion by awarding Spen King a one-month salary bonus and a fortnight's salary bonus to other employees who had taken part in the trials. Peter Wilks' organisation fee was £500 – which was a quite substantial sum in 1952 and equates to about £18,500 in 2023 figures. And, of course, Rover once again made publicity capital out of JET 1's achievements.

The car next appeared in public in November 1952, when it was driven by Geoffrey Lloyd, then Minister for Fuel and Power, who no doubt felt obliged to acquire some knowledge of what looked like a viable new form of automotive propulsion. By this time, JET 1 had been fitted with a new full-width frameless perspex windscreen and with a small vertical perspex screen behind the seats, designed to shield the occupants from the exhaust gases, which emerged vertically a few feet behind their heads. It had also been fitted with sidelights just below the headlamps to make it road-legal in Britain.

JET 1 then disappeared back to Solihull, where its creators now focused on the various problems that faced the car gas turbine programme. One was to make a gas turbine car that more closely resembled a conventional petrol-engined type. As Maurice Wilks had told the press at the Silverstone event in March 1950, 'in any future production car we would certainly not put the engine where one expects to find the back seat.' The attempts to create such a car are explained below. However, there were also two major technical problems.

JET 1 was later given side-lights to make it road-legal. It survives in the Science Museum in London.

Technical Problems

One was the need for a heat exchanger that could lower the operating temperature of the engine, and the difficulty there was that a suitable material from which to make such a thing simply did not exist at the time. The second problem was of poor fuel consumption, which would have been alleviated if a heat exchanger had been available. Unfortunately, 4mpg (59l/100km)was not practicable for a road car. The issue here was not so much the cost of the fuel, as paraffin was not then taxed, but of the need to provide an enormous onboard fuel tank to give the gas turbine car a reasonable range.

The gas turbine car was not seen again in public until 1958, when Rover presented it to the Science Museum in London on permanent loan. JET 1 was delivered to London by lorry, but was driven through the entrance to the museum under its own power. Since then, it has been driven just once – when it did some exhibition laps at Silverstone on 20 July 1963, together with the later T3, T4 and Rover-BRM experimental gas turbine cars. Nevertheless, when interviewed in the mid-1990s, Spen King was convinced that he could get it to run again ... if only someone would give him the chance!

JET 1's real long-term value to Rover was that it publicised the innovative engineering abilities of

The car's metallic paint finish has sometimes led to suggestions that it was grey. It was photographed here in 2012 at a classic car show.

a company that up to that point had been largely seen as conservative and staid. Even though the Rover name would be reassuringly associated with conservative values for many more years, this new image would prove very helpful in boosting public confidence in the brand. There was, somehow, something very British about the potential lurking behind the discreet public image, and Rover's clear ability to innovate suggested that the company had a sound future ahead of it.

The T2 Saloon

The second gas turbine car prototype was planned as a standard P4 saloon with its engine mounted conventionally under the bonnet at the front. This of course raised the question of how the exhaust gases were going to be vented into the atmosphere. A simple exhaust system like that used on the production cars was going to be completely inadequate for the large volume of exhaust gases produced by a gas turbine engine. Somebody then came up with the idea of enlarging the chassis side-members and running the exhaust through these. So, by the middle of February 1951, Gordon Bashford was drawing up the special chassis for the car that was to be called T2.

Bashford's notebook does not show the actual dimensions of the new side-members, but he remembered them many years later as being something like 9 inches deep; or more than twice as deep as those of the standard P4 chassis. No pictures of the car are known, but pictures of its later incarnation as T2A confirm the extra depth of the chassis rails. They show that the jacking-points welded to their undersides were some inches below the body sills instead of right up against them, as on the production cars. The car also had double bumpers at front and rear, which was probably the easiest way of concealing the non-standard relationship between body and chassis frame.

As space in the engine bay was limited, Rover decided not to use the T8 turbine that had powered JET 1 but to fit a smaller T6 engine, which had a 6-inch diameter compressor turbine. With 120bhp at a compressor speed of 50,000rpm, this had more than enough power for an everyday road car. This second gas turbine car was built to resemble a 1952-season P4 saloon, and was road-registered as MAC 273 on 25 March 1952. By the time of the Jabbeke speed runs with JET 1 in June it had 'run among everyday English traffic without exciting any particular comment', according to *The Autocar* dated 4 July 1952.

The public may not have passed comment, but the engineers most certainly did. The biggest problem was that unburnt paraffin tended to collect in the chassis side-members during the engine's ignition cycle, and would then suddenly ignite once the engine was running and produce huge clouds of smoke. To prevent worse disasters, the Rover engineers added extensive lagging around the side members, but in the end they were forced to accept that the solution was impracticable. Engineer Noel Penny believed (in *Automotive Gas Turbines* by John Mortimer) that T2 became a 'white elephant' and may have influenced Frank Bell's decision to leave Rover.

Of some interest is that the Rover company record for this car shows its identification number as XT3, rather than the XT2 that might be expected as a follow-up to the XT1 number allocated to JET 1. There is no known explanation for this, but a possibility is that the handwritten record was completed after T2 had been converted to T2A and that it was therefore re-numbered as a third prototype. There certainly was no other car involved in the sequence, as Spen King confirmed in an interview with the author in the mid-1990s.

The T2A Saloon

Rather than scrap T2 altogether and start again, the Rover gas turbine engineers rebuilt it to a different design. This time, they put the engine in the boot, and replaced the boot lid by a huge vertical funnel that carried the exhaust

The second gas turbine car had its engine at the front, but that caused problems. This is almost certainly it, with a cloth and tape mock-up of the proposed exhaust funnel for its second incarnation with a rear-mounted engine. The position of the jacking points makes the extra depth of the chassis obvious.

Here fully rebuilt as T2A, the car shows the huge exhaust stack that almost completely concealed the engine from view.

The rear window was enlarged to fit around the exhaust funnel, and just visible on the engine 'lid' is a 'Rover' script badge – almost certainly adapted from that for a Rover 90.

gases up to roof level. As this blocked off most of the rear window, they designed a wrap-around window to fit on either side of it, and the whole design was mocked-up on the car, using what appears to be paper or possibly cloth.

Once that was satisfactory, metal was cut and shaped appropriately. T2 became T2A, still sitting on T2's deeper chassis with its double bumpers and wearing its MAC 273 registration number. Its engine was once again a T6 gas turbine – quite possibly the same one that had earlier been fitted at the front – and according to the written record was numbered T6/12. There was still no heat exchanger, as Rover had still not come up with a satisfactory design. The engine drove forward to what appears to have been a modified Land-Rover transfer gearbox in the conventional position, and the drive was then taken back to the rear axle along a conventional propellor shaft. As with JET1 and T2, there was no clutch and there were no gears.

T2A was probably completed in 1954, and in *The Motor* for 26 September 1956, there is a reference to restricted information having been released about the car that year. No trace of any press release has so far come to light, however. Spen King later explained that there was no major release of information to the press about T2 and T2A because 'they were both fairly embarrassing. Nobody wanted anybody to see them very much'. A small picture of T2A did accompany *The Motor* article about the new T3 gas turbine car in September 1956, but by then the car itself had probably been scrapped.

Rover Gas Turbines Ltd

Although the primary focus of Rover's gas turbine work was on developing a gas turbine road car, as early as autumn 1950 the company took a first look at alternative uses for the technology. As explained above, managing director S. B. Wilks owned a former motor torpedo boat named *Torquil* (it was not a yacht, as the Rover Board minutes had it), and he had the company's gas turbines team replace its engines with a pair of T8 engines. Noel Penny (in John Mortimer's book, *Automotive Gas Turbines*) remembered these as delivering 200bhp each and that the boat was then tested on the River Thames.

There was some precedent for this. The Admiralty had shown an interest in gas turbine power as early as 1947, when they had experimentally installed a 2,500hp engine made by Metropolitan Vickers in a gunboat. Perhaps Rover believed there might be a commercial opportunity here, and Noel Penny recalled that the Admiralty bought several T8 engines, which they put through endurance tests at their AEL experimental establishment in West Drayton. Rover certainly was keen to pursue the Admiralty interest, and the Board minutes record that the two T8 engines in *Torquil* were replaced by a pair of Rover Meteorite V8 engines towards the end of 1951 and that there was potential interest from the Admiralty. (There is more about the Meteorite V8 engine in Appendix V.)

The T8s, though, were large gas turbine engines, and Rover also saw the potential to exploit their work commercially by developing a small portable gas turbine engine that could be used to power fire pumps, generators and so on. Work initially focused on an engine codenamed Neptune, a small single-shaft turbine. The company attracted interest from the Ministry of Supply quite early on, a condition of the contract being that MoS representatives would become involved in shaping the requirement. Noel Penny (in *Automotive Gas Turbines*) remembered that there were arguments about whether to use a radial turbine in place of the axial type in Rover's existing designs. The axial design won the day, and the new engine was brought to production as the 1S/60 type (single-shaft, 60bhp).

Rover's chairman, Ransom Harrison, advised the company's shareholders of developments in his statement to the Annual General Meeting of 19 December 1952. 'We are finding,' he said, 'that there is likely to be a market for small gas turbine engines for industrial and service purposes.' A re-organisation of the old gas turbine department soon followed, and during 1953 it became a separate legal entity as Rover Gas Turbines Ltd. The main reason for the change was that it allowed sales and marketing appropriate to the products, and separated them from the existing Rover sales organisation that was geared to selling cars. Geoffrey Searle, already a Rover director, became head of the new company.

Further changes ensued when Frank Bell decided to leave; by mid-March 1953 he had been appointed chief engine designer for the Blackburn Aircraft Company. Noel Penny says that Stewart Hambling was brought in to replace him, but that Hambling later left to set up a gas turbine department at Standard-Triumph, and poached a few of the Rover gas turbine staff at the same time. Spen King had already taken charge of gas turbine research, and his cousin Peter Wilks now returned to Rover from his time with the dealers Gethin's to become production manager for Rover Gas Turbines Ltd.

The 1S/60 gas turbine entered production in late 1954. Spen King told Graham Bannock (author of *Range Rover, The Creators of an Icon*) that he promised to approve its production if the gas turbine team could demonstrate its reliability in a 200-hour full-power test. The final prototype met the criteria. The market was slow at first, although the longer-term future appeared more promising thanks to the MoS interest, which turned out to have been for an auxiliary power plant on the Vulcan bomber that was then under development (*see* sidebar).

Better marketing seems to have been the key to wider success, and by 1956 Rover were offering the 1S/60 as the central element in a series of purpose-designed packages. It could be bought with a Rotax 3-phase electrical generator, a BTH alternator, a Petbow generator, a Sigmund 500gpm pump or as an Instructional Set for

VULCAN AAPP (AIRBORNE AUXILIARY POWER PLANT)

Perhaps the best-known use of Rover's 1S/60 gas turbine engine was as the AAPP (Airborne Auxiliary Power Plant) aboard the Avro Vulcan bomber. Deliveries of the Vulcan to the RAF began in September 1956.

The AAPP, a Gas Turbine Mk 10301 in the military canon, was mounted in a cradle. Its purpose was to provide an emergency electricity supply of 200 volts at altitudes below 30,000ft. This would be needed in the unlikely event that all four engines stalled and all four alternators therefore ceased to supply power for the aircraft's controls. The AAPP was under the control of the Air Electronics Officer and was located outboard of no 4 engine. It could be started either electrically or by a cartridge.

The Vulcan's AAPP had no throttle control and was designed to run at a constant speed. It had its own oxygen supply that was carried in two bottles mounted at the rear of the engine. On the ground, the AAPP could also be used to provide power and air for the ventilated suits worn by the crew.

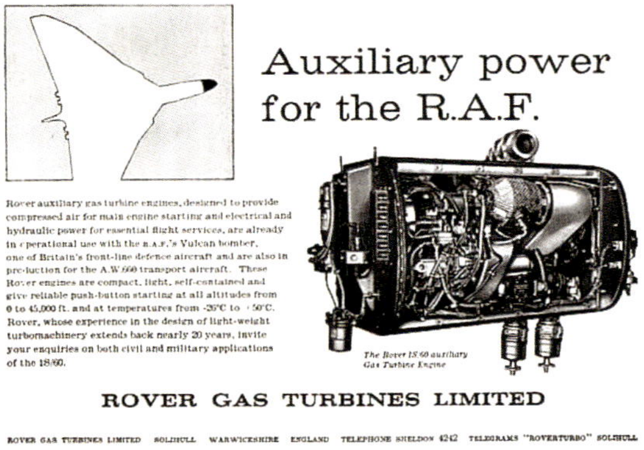

Rover's move in to gas turbine engines for other purposes was greatly aided by an order from the RAF for an AAPU to be used in the new Vulcan bomber.

This AAPU from a Vulcan bomber is seen without its protective mounting cage.

This picture taken from a sales brochure for the later 1S/60 engine shows that the 60bhp gas turbine engine was a quarter of the size of a 60bhp Rover 60 petrol engine.

The Duke of Edinburgh (centre) visited Rover's Solihull factory in early 1958. Among other things, he was shown this gas turbine-powered portable fire pump. On his right in the suit is Maurice Wilks, and on the right of the picture is George Farmer. Just visible in front of the building behind them is a Road Rover prototype, probably RR11.

This portable fire pump powered by a Rover gas turbine unit was demonstrated at a Rover enthusiasts' gathering in New Zealand in 2012.

universities and technical colleges, when it was mounted on a bedplate with a Heenan & Froude dynamometer. The sales brochure incorporated a striking picture comparing the size of a 60bhp 1S/60 gas turbine engine with a 60bhp Rover 60 petrol engine, which, without its gearbox, was four times as heavy as the gas turbine engine.

As Graham Bannock put it:

> *the selling point was that 60bhp... of pump capacity could be carried easily by two people – for example by naval ratings from one part of the ship to another. These sets were used by almost every navy in Europe.*

He also noted that:

> *some of the less exotic uses of these 'commercial' gas turbine sets included driving machinery to suck out sand in a Lancashire quarry. In Greenland, making use of both drive power and exhaust, Rover turbines were used to drive a fish mill and cook the fish.*

However, it is important not to over-state the success of the Rover gas turbine venture. It did indeed survive into the early 1970s, latterly being transferred to the Alvis company, which Rover bought out in 1965, but it often failed to meet its own costs and, in Noel Penny's estimation, probably just about broke even over its entire lifetime.

CHAPTER 7

Revolution: The Land-Rover

Rover's longer-term future was far from clear at the start of 1947. Cars were coming off the assembly lines at a reasonable rate and volumes were gradually increasing despite the hindrances and setbacks caused by continuing materials shortages. New engines and a new chassis design were well underway, but, as Chapters 4 and 5 explain, progress on the eventual new model had been held up by problems with the body design.

The gas turbine development work was slowly moving forward, but it was far too soon to base any longer-term plans around it. The work on a second new model range, the small M Model, was beginning to look as if it might be a dead end. Worse was the government's insistence on exports. Rover were trying hard to get a foothold in overseas markets and had enjoyed some success, but they simply did not have a model in production that was appealing to more than a small percentage of potential customers. Nor did they have such a model in the pipeline.

Rover management had probably heard stories and rumours about what other British manufacturers were doing and, although such snippets of information were not to be trusted in their entirety, they would have been a constant reminder that the clock was ticking. The unusually severe winter conditions that led to country-wide power shortages and to a need to close the production lines for a large part of February cannot have offered any comfort. The pressure on Rover management must therefore have been quite intense, and although their approach was probably calm and measured, it is hard to imagine that they did not consider the whole position to be very worrying.

There were even domestic consequences for chief engineer Maurice Wilks, as many of the trees in the long drive leading up to his home at Blackdown Manor near Leamington Spa blew down, making access to the main road difficult. His response was to visit a nearby military surplus dump and buy a Lloyd carrier – a small tracked vehicle that was undaunted by mud or snow and was able to drag the fallen trees out of the way.

Not long after that, his neighbour – a Colonel Nash – showed Wilks the army surplus Jeep he had bought. Wilks was fascinated by it, and before long the two men agreed to swap vehicles. The Jeep, registered FWD 734, became Maurice Wilks' new plaything some time around February 1947, quite probably during the period of power shortages. He used it to clear more trees at Blackdown Manor, and later on he would take

The inspiration for the Land-Rover came from a war surplus Jeep that Maurice Wilks acquired. This picture from home cine film (colour was rare in those days) shows him with his family and the Jeep on Anglesey, where the family had a holiday cottage.

it off to the cottage he had bought as a holiday home on Anglesey. Home cine film from the time shows him using it to tow and launch a boat on the sands at nearby Red Wharf Bay, and – in typical Maurice Wilks fashion – thoroughly enjoying himself at the same time.

As an engineer, Wilks quite naturally took an interest in how the Jeep worked, and before long he was beginning to wonder whether Rover could build a similar vehicle using existing production components. It could be designed and put into production quite quickly, as no expensive press tools would be required, and a very simple body could be manufactured by hand. Wilks was more than likely aware that Willys had turned their wartime military model into a maid-of-all-work over in the USA, where the Jeep CJ-2A was proving attractive to farmers and others who worked on the land. He clearly realised that such a vehicle would have a strong appeal overseas as well as in Britain, and might be exactly what Rover needed to keep themselves going until better times returned.

At Easter 1947, Maurice Wilks and family went to stay at their holiday cottage on Anglesey. The family's nanny, Kathleen Griffith, clearly remembered many years later that they were on the beach at Red Wharf Bay one day, and that S. B. Wilks joined them. Maurice sketched out in the sand his ideas for a Rover version of the civilian Jeep. This episode, which Kathleen Griffith related to Land-Rover author John Smith for his book *Land-Rover, The Formative Years, 1947–1967*, has unfortunately been heavily romanticised by Land-Rover's public relations staff in more recent years to the point where its veracity has been called into question. Realistically, what probably happened is that Maurice Wilks simply sketched

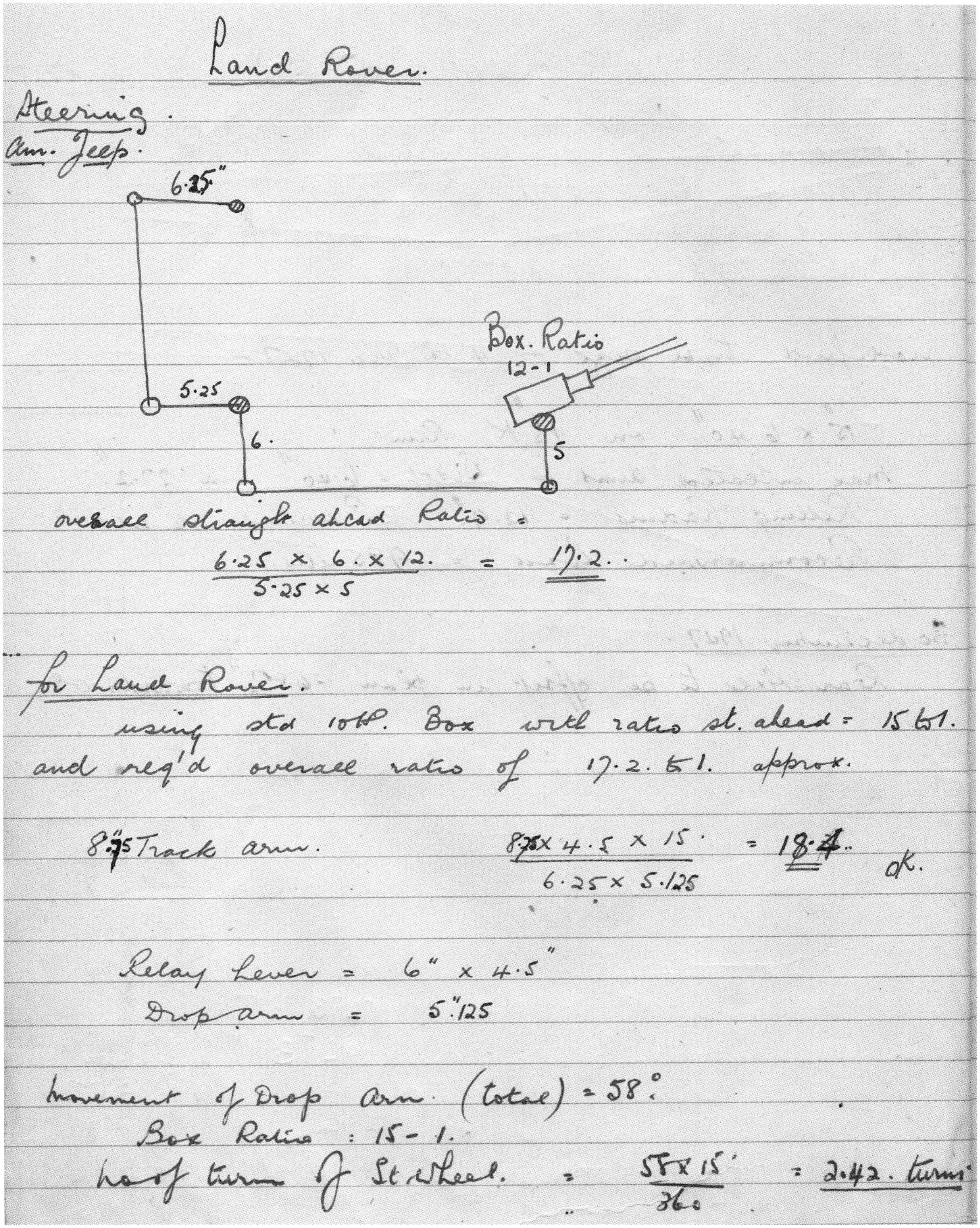

Land Rover.

Steering.
Am. Jeep.

overall straight ahead Ratio =

$$\frac{6.25 \times 6. \times 12.}{5.25 \times 5} = 17.2..$$

for Land Rover.

using std 10HP. Box with ratio st. ahead = 15 to 1.
and req'd overall ratio of 17.2. to 1. approx.

8.75 Track arm. $\frac{8.75 \times 4.5 \times 15.}{6.25 \times 5.125} = 18.4..$ ok.

Relay Lever = 6" × 4.5"
Drop arm = 5".125

Movement of Drop arm (total) = 58°.
Box Ratio : 15 - 1.
No of turns of St Wheel. = $\frac{58 \times 15}{360}$ = 2.42. turns

Once the basic idea was in place, Rover's design engineers set to work. This page is from Gordon Bashford's notebook, and shows calculations relating to the steering. Note the reference to 'Am(erican) Jeep'.

something like a plan view of the vehicle in the sand, to show his brother how the four-wheel-drive transmission system would be laid out.

Over the next few months, he continued to work up these ideas, and by the time of the Rover Board meeting on 3 September 1947, the Wilks brothers were sure that this was the product they wanted as a second line alongside the familiar middle-class Rover saloons. The record of that Board meeting explains very simply what the thinking was. S. B. Wilks said that:

> *... of the various alternatives that had been under consideration, he was of the opinion that the all-purpose vehicle on the lines of the Willys Overland post-war Jeep was the most desirable. The P3 engine, gearbox and back axle could be used almost in their entirety.*

He added that the development department had already carried out considerable research on this vehicle:

> *It was, therefore, agreed that this should be sanctioned for production.*

A Formal Programme

The decision to go ahead with production of this 'all-purpose vehicle' was very much a pragmatic one. It could hardly have been more radically different from the discreet, refined saloon models on which Rover's reputation had been built. A few eyebrows must have been raised at Board level, and a few eyes must have been rolled further down the management chain, but these were extraordinary times and they demanded extraordinary solutions. Everybody at Rover knew that the decision to go ahead had been made by the same people who had saved the Rover company from almost certain failure just over a decade earlier, and they would have trusted their judgement.

By the time of that Board meeting in early September, the timescale for design and development was looking very tight indeed. Maurice Wilks must have been aware of industry talk about a resumption of motor shows in the first few months of 1948. As export sales were critical to the whole concept of this new model, it would have to be announced at a European motor show rather than at the Earl's Court one in the autumn. The dates of those shows were not yet settled, but the major one was likely to be the one in Geneva, which had traditionally been held in late February or early March. If a production-ready vehicle was to be displayed there, Rover had about six months to complete the design.

That was a very tall order. The normal design and development process might be short-circuited by using readily available components from the cars, and the body might be easy to get into production by using hand fabrication in place of machine tools, but the whole project needed to be driven forward by somebody with the right qualities. That somebody could not be Maurice Wilks himself, because he had too many other things to be doing.

Arthur Goddard was the engineer chosen to take the Land-Rover from idea to production.

Finding the right engineer to oversee the new project was therefore critical, and Wilks was very lucky indeed to have a strong candidate already on his staff. Arthur Goddard was a forceful and determined young engineer who had impressed Wilks with his ability to get things done when he had sorted out a timing chain problem on the OHV engines while Jack Swaine was absent after breaking both legs in a motorcycling accident. Under Goddard, John Cullen was appointed as the project's chief development engineer, and in the meantime five section leaders in the drawing office were set to work on different areas of the design. All this, of course, was additional to the work that they and their staffs were doing to get the new P3 saloons ready for introduction in the first quarter of 1948.

Maurice Wilks, of course, was very much a hands-on engineer, and there was never any chance that he would simply let his staff get on with the job and focus his attentions elsewhere. He had to get involved somehow, and as a side project while the drawing office got on with their work, Wilks lost no time in creating a 'mule' prototype to get some early ideas of how his concept might work out in practice. The simple solution was to start by putting a Rover engine into a wartime Jeep, and entries in the Toft-Bate photographic record make clear that work was being done on a chassis and engine by the last week in September 1947.

The Centre-Steer

Whether this hybrid ever had a Rover engine and a Jeep body at the same time is questionable, as by the end of September the whole thing was being built up in the jig shop at Rover with a new hand-made body. One of the key characteristics of this 'mule' prototype was that it had its steering wheel in the centre, and as a result it became known as the 'Centre-Steer'. Photographs show, incidentally, that the host Jeep was a Willys MB rather than a Ford GPW. It had the tubular front chassis cross-member used only on that version of the wartime vehicle.

Central to Wilks' plan was to give the Land-Rover a version of the new IOE engine that was about to enter production for the P3 saloon cars. It must therefore have been a prototype of one of these that went into the Centre-Steer. Gordon Bashford told author Graham Robson many years ago that he believed it was a 10hp engine, and this has led many commentators to assume that it was the 10hp OHV engine from the Rover Ten then in production.

It was almost certainly not. First, to use such an engine would have been nonsensical when there were prototypes of the new IOE engine already in existence. Second, it is clear from pictures of the Centre-Steer that the exhaust system ran along the left-hand side of the chassis, which is consistent with the use of an IOE engine; the OHV engines had their exhaust emerging on the right of the engine and therefore the main system would have run along that side of the chassis. So if Gordon Bashford's recollection of a 10hp engine was correct, the most likely explanation is that this was a 10hp IOE prototype. Perhaps such an engine was more readily available than the 12hp type that was eventually chosen, as the 10hp had been rejected as a production option for the cars some time earlier. Though doubtless less powerful than the 12hp type, it would have been physically almost identical and good enough to prove the concept.

That impractical central steering position would go on to catch the imagination of historians and commentators alike, but it was originally intended as a very practical solution to the problem of creating vehicles for export. Clearly, both RHD and LHD versions would be needed, and Wilks appears to have thought that a central steering position would satisfy both requirements and would reduce both costs and complication on the assembly lines. Quite possibly, he was also thinking that farmers were among the target customers for the new vehicle, and that they were already used to a central steering posi-

Maurice Wilks wanted to test out his ideas on a 'mule' vehicle while the drawing office worked out the production design. This is not the real thing, but a lovingly crafted replica of the Centre Steer.

The driving position in the Centre Steer was far from ideal...

... and when the hood was erected, the driver's hand signals were invisible to following drivers.

tion in a tractor. He achieved what he wanted by leaving the Jeep's steering box in position and running a roller chain from it to the centrally-mounted steering column.

It was one of those great ideas that did not work out as planned. The centrally located steering column required an uncomfortable splayed-legs driving position, as the clutch was on its left while the brake and accelerator were on the right. It also became clear that, when the canvas hood was erected, following traffic could not see the driver's hand signals (for turning and slowing down) that were still in everyday use in the late 1940s.

The Centre-Steer was a pure Maurice Wilks project, produced quite independently of the main development programme that Wilks had entrusted to Arthur Goddard. When interviewed about it many years later, Goddard was quite dismissive of the vehicle. It did not contribute materially to the development of the eventual production Land-Rover, but it did satisfy Maurice Wilks that his concept would work. Once that function had been achieved, it was simply redundant, and the last official photographs of it were taken on 28 January 1948.

There have of course been several 'sightings' of the legendary Centre-Steer vehicle in more recent years, but there can be little doubt that it was eventually scrapped. Maurice Wilks' son Stephen told John Smith that his father once took him round the factory and pointed out 'a pile of light alloy body parts by a wall, telling him quite clearly that they had belonged to the very first Land-Rover.' There have also been some claims that there were actually two Centre-Steer vehicles, despite the absence of any convincing supporting evidence. Why Rover might actually have needed more than one is of course much harder to explain. One thing that can be said for certain is that there are now more Centre-Steers than Rover ever built, as dedicated enthusiasts have created replica vehicles on the basis of surviving photographs.

The Origins of the Name

The new model already had a name by the time of the Rover Board meeting in September 1947, and this was recorded in the minutes as 'Landrover'. It appears that this was not a prototype of the eventual spelling: the patent agents had advised the company to register the name as a single word because the two-word derivative would then also be covered. Under patent law, the separated form of the name was considered as a variant of the basic registered name. So the name was duly registered as Landrover at the Patent Office on 11 October 1947 under number 663199.

According to the late Richard Wilks, a nephew of Rover's two Wilks brothers, that name was dreamed up over the summer of 1947 on Islay, the little island in the Hebrides off the coast of Scotland, where S. B. Wilks owned a holiday retreat. Wilks went out one morning to walk up grouse on the moors with his son Thomas and nephew Richard. They had stopped for a lunch of beer and sandwiches, and S. B. mentioned that he had left instructions for the engineering department at Solihull to have a Rover engine and gearbox in a Jeep on his return from holiday. There was no name for the new vehicle yet.

Richard Wilks promptly suggested Roverlander. This incorporated the name of the company satisfactorily and gave some indication of the vehicle's intended purpose. However, his uncle objected that it sounded too much like the name of the Jeep's manufacturer – Willys Overland. Thomas Wilks then suggested calling it the Landrover. And that name stuck, although before production began it would become two hyphenated words as Land-Rover, no doubt to stress the link with the Rover company. (The hyphen was progressively dropped after the formation of Land Rover Ltd in 1978, but was always present in the early days.)

A Ruthlessly Rational Design

Among those five section leaders in the drawing office who had been given the job of designing the new Land-Rover was Gordon Bashford. His job was to design the new chassis frame, and he remembered many years later that one of his first tasks was to visit a military surplus dump somewhere in the Cotswolds and to buy four Jeeps so that the Rover design team could take them apart and discover what made them tick. Bashford decided to use box-section side members rather than the Jeep's channel-section members, which were notoriously prone to cracking. The box section would give vital extra strength, and Rover was already wedded to the idea of using the same principle for its forthcoming 1948 cars.

Work on the engine fell to Joe Drinkwater, who had to adapt Rover's brand-new 1595cc four-cylinder IOE type to suit its new role in the proposed utility vehicle. Transmission design was allocated to Tom Barton, a no-nonsense ex-railway engineer, and his main job was to draw up a two-speed transfer gearbox to bolt onto the existing Rover car gearbox and give the Land-Rover crawler ratios for driving across rough terrain. Barton was quite young at the time, and his work was overseen by Frank Shaw, head of the transmissions team. It was probably Shaw who suggested using the freewheel from existing Rover cars to prevent problems of transmission wind-up between the front and rear axles.

The two-speed transfer gearbox had an additional function as well. It incorporated a power take-off (PTO) like that on a tractor so that the Land-Rover could be used as a stationary power source to drive farm machinery. This was a very important element in Maurice Wilks' vision of the vehicle that was designed to increase its adaptability and potential usefulness. There had been at least one PTO on the Centre-Steer vehicle, mounted on the rear chassis cross-member and

The 1595cc engine was standard until mid-1950.

driven by a shaft from the gearbox; the Centre-Steer was also dummied up with a capstan winch that would have been driven by a front PTO if it had actually had one.

The fifth section leader on Maurice Wilks' design team was Sam Ostler, an experienced body engineer whose job was to come up with the bodywork for the new vehicle. This was no easy task, because design of the body was constrained by the need for simplicity. Rover did not want to go to the expense of having new body tooling made, even if they were able to find a company to make it for them in the time-scale they had in mind. So a guiding principle was that the body panels were to be flat or, at the most, to have a single curvature so that they could be formed by hand. Rigidity was to be achieved by using angle-iron to form the basic shape of the body and by riveting the panels to this.

As the new vehicle was aimed at farmers and others who were likely to use it in severe conditions and leave it outside for most of the time, structural durability was also important. Rover chose to use corrosion-resistant panels made from Birmabright aluminium alloy, which was produced by Birmal in the Midlands and was actually easier to obtain than steel, which was rationed at this stage. Also to resist corrosion, the plan was to have exposed steelwork galvanised, which meant the body's 'frame' components (usually described as 'cappings') and also the chassis frame. In practice, the galvanised chassis frame would be abandoned after about 150–200 production vehicles had been made, probably mainly to save costs and streamline assembly.

The Centre-Steer prototype had been finished in grey, perhaps largely because there were

THE CLEAN DESIGN OF THE LAND-ROVER CHASSIS . . .

THIS view of the Land-Rover Chassis shows its clean serviceable design. The drive for the centre and rear power take-off is taken through the main gearbox and the drive to the front and rear axles is from the transfer box. The chassis frame is of box section and exceptionally strong. The Land-Rover is not an adapted vehicle, it is specially designed and built to cover a wide field of usefulness in the service of agriculture and industry.

The Land-Rover chassis was designed to be both rugged and simple to build. This illustration comes from a 1950 sales brochure and shows it with a rear-mounted power take-off that was driven by a propshaft from the back of the transfer gearbox.

supplies of that colour paint around at the time: in the difficult post-war conditions, the engineers would have used what they had to hand rather than held out for something more attractive. However, grey was undoubtedly drab, and it was probably Maurice Wilks who wanted something more eye-catching to help sell the vehicle. Once again, it looks as if he chose from what was to hand. Rover were already ordering quantities of an attractive light-green colour for the P3 saloons that had entered production in January, and this would be ideal for a vehicle that would be used in the country as a farm runabout. In tandem with green leather upholstery, it was listed in Rover catalogues as 'No 2 Green', and that name remained in use when the colour combination was adopted for the Land-Rover – although in this case washable leathercloth was selected for the upholstery.

The Pre-Production Batch

By the start of 1948, a temporary production line had been laid down in a corner of the assembly shop at Solihull, in the building now known as the South Works, and work had begun on a planned batch of 50 pre-production models. This was a much higher number of prototypes than Rover normally built and was a reflection of their need to test a large number of new features in a very short time; this was, after all, a very different type of vehicle from the comfortable saloon cars that were traditional Rover fare. In practice, only 48 pre-production Land-Rovers were built, and supposedly for the very good reason that the engineers did not need any more. By the time the last few were completed, production models had begun to roll off the assembly lines, and any further development work could be more profitably and easily done on some of them.

Not only were assembly procedures being tried out on this pre-production batch, but so were many of the design features. As a result, there were multiple changes of specification during the six months or so of pre-production assembly, and early vehicles were typically updated with later design features as the process went on. As the necessary tooling had not yet been made, many items on these vehicles were hand-fabricated, and surviving examples still bear such features as bronze pedals.

Notable changes in the specification during this period included some to the transmissions, which on the earliest examples had four push-pull controls that ran through the dashboard; these were later changed to floor-mounted levers and a ring-pull for the freewheel. Some had a permanent four-wheel-drive transmission, and others had a selectable type; some were changed from one to the other and retained features from both. To meet demand from the development engineers, some pre-production models were changed from LHD to RHD or vice versa.

The first pre-production Land-Rover appears to have been completed in March 1948, and it was given the identity number R01. The R simply stood for right-hand drive, just as it did on Rover cars, and those examples built with left-hand drive had an L identifying prefix. All 48 examples were numbered sequentially, and in cases where the steering position was changed, the chassis retained its original serial number but was re-stamped with the appropriate prefix letter.

Those working on the Land-Rover project must have been under quite severe pressure in the early months of 1948. Top management wanted to launch the vehicle at the Geneva motor show that was scheduled for March, but it soon became clear that this was out of the question because no vehicles were likely to be completed in time. Design and development were progressing more or less in tandem at what must have felt like a glacially slow pace.

With Geneva ruled out as an option, Rover settled for the next motor show on the 1948 calendar, which was to open in Amsterdam at the end of April. Even by that time, only a very limited number of pre-production models had been completed, and from them Rover chose two with

This wonderful old photograph shows the very first Land-Rover (the number 1 is painted on its rear cross-member) being tested in the ford on the Packington Estate. John Cullen is driving, and Arthur Goddard is in the passenger seat.

That first Land-Rover still survives and is owned by JLR. It has been restored and re-restored to make it as close as possible to the way it was built.

The Land-Rover on the stand at Amsterdam was L05, equipped as a mobile welder. The loops on the tailgate were designed to support gas bottles, but the design was changed before production began.

Pilot vehicle R06 was equipped as a fire engine. Here it is at an early stage of development, showing the Pegson fire pump and an interesting plate bearing a version of the Land-Rover logo that was not pursued.

R06 was further developed to produce this neat-looking machine. Production types differed again.

left-hand drive. These were numbers L03 (which became the demonstrator at the show) and L05, which was on the stand inside the exhibition hall. L05 was equipped as a mobile welder, a variant that Rover believed would sell well. (The story that a third vehicle, L07, was also present at Amsterdam appears to be purely wishful thinking, made up by public relations staff after Land-Rover had obtained the remains of L07 in 2016.)

By the time of the Amsterdam show, no badges had been made for the Land-Rover, although a logo or motif had been designed. This was displayed on the front wing of L03 (but not L05) and was a large casting that consisted of the words 'Land' and 'Rover', one above the other and linked by a Z-shaped flash. It is said to have been inspired by the way Rover draughtsman Larry Watts used to sign his name; Maurice Wilks saw it, liked it, and copied it for the company's new vehicle. An oval die-cast badge with a border around the logo was drawn up in May, but before this entered production many vehicles were fitted with a borderless oval brass casting. The borderless castings were not painted; the later ones initially had red letters and border on a background that matched the body colour, until the red was changed for yellow later in 1948.

Some of the 48 pre-production Land-Rovers were used as demonstrators before production volumes had built up, and inevitably Rover modified these so that they were representative of the latest production standard. Two (numbers

L29 and R30) were evaluated by the Ministry of Supply, which was then the purchasing agency for Britain's armed forces, and this would lead to large military orders later on. Two more (numbers L31 and R32) went to the National Institute for Agricultural Engineering, which wanted to test how well they really performed as agricultural vehicles.

Three more went to Rover's overseas representatives to help spread the knowledge of the new product, and four were temporarily exported to Europe for much the same reason. A few were sold to Rover employees when they were no longer needed for development work, and no doubt any damaged parts were replaced by current production items either at that stage or later on during ownership. Each one of the survivors has its own tale to tell, but probably not one of them is today in its original build condition.

Success

The Land-Rover seems to have created something of a sensation at the Amsterdam show, and Rover soon found itself inundated with enquiries and firm orders. There was military interest, too, as the Jeep's success during wartime had made clear how useful a nimble four-wheel-drive runabout could be. By the time full production began in June, orders were coming in from around the world and it was clear that Maurice Wilks' idea had more potential than even he had imagined. By the end of the year, the Rover chairman was telling shareholders that it seemed likely the Land-Rover would become far more important to the company than had earlier been envisaged.

Production gradually built up. Just 3,000 Land-Rovers were built in the first twelve months as 1948 models (for the exact dates of the model-year, please *see* the table in Chapter 1). A further 5,000 were built in the first half of the following year as 1949 models; and then 15,949 for the 1950 model-year. That this success had taken Rover by surprise was clear from the fact that production of the basic models exceeded the 9,999 allowed for under the original chassis numbering system for the 1950 model-year, and so a new numbering series had to be started.

Export was the name of the game in the beginning, and Rover made sure that its efforts gained adequate publicity!

S. B. Wilks (with the handkerchief in his pocket) shows an early Land-Rover demonstration chassis to Lord Mountbatten. These early chassis were painted silver.

A few more figures help to illustrate the scale of the Land-Rover's success. By the end of 1949 the company was able to boast that it was selling Land-Rovers in more than 70 different countries around the world, and that exports were absorbing 75–80 per cent of Land-Rover production. By June 1950, around 350 Land-Rovers were rolling off the production lines every week – a figure that represented an increase in production volumes of 250 per cent in just under two years! As the new decade began, production was increasing to meet orders that seemed never to stop coming in. As the motoring world gradually returned to normal, so the material supply restrictions that had blighted the Land-Rover's early days were easing as well.

Production Changes, 1948–51

More than 60 years after the events described here, Land-Rover project leader Arthur Goddard admitted that the shortage of time between concept and production meant that Rover had to introduce the vehicle first and develop it later! So it should come as no surprise that there were multiple minor specification changes and a few more major ones in the first few months of production. In fact there would be dozens of minor changes over the lifetime of the 1.6-litre models, as Rover made modifications in response to feedback from its customers.

This is not the place to list all of them, but it is useful to highlight a few in order to give a flavour of what was happening. Only 1,300 Land-Rovers had the original 4.88:1 differentials, which were taken from stocks made for the 10hp and 12hp Rover cars that went out of production at the end of 1947. The new P3 saloons that had been announced just before the Land-Rover in February 1948 had a 4.7:1 axle ratio, and the Land-Rover switched to this as soon as stocks of the older items dried up, which must have been around November 1948. A month and 200 Land-Rovers later, the original five-leaf road springs gave way to stronger six-leaf springs, and the original angular gearbox cover was changed for a more rounded type to accompany the change from a body-mounted gear lever to a gearbox-mounted one.

The P3 saloons had a further effect on the Land-Rover at the beginning of the 1949 model-year (for dates, *see* the table in Chapter 1), when their four-spoke steering wheel replaced the original two-spoke type that had come from the earlier cars. June brought the option of a full-width scuttle ventilator, a hinged panel below the windscreen that allowed a flow of air directly into the vehicle. But the early summer was perhaps more noteworthy for some colour changes.

The changes began in May, when the matt silver chassis paint was changed to the same light green as the body, but around 1,500 vehicles later there was a further and more permanent change when both body and chassis changed to the Bronze Green that would for many years be the archetypal Land-Rover colour. The usual explanation for this is that the British army's first bulk order began to come off the lines in June, and that it was finished in the Bronze Green (strictly Deep Bronze Green) that was the standard 'peacetime' livery for army vehicles.

PTOs (Power Take-Offs) added to the Land-Rover's versatility. This rear PTO is fitted with a pulley that drove a belt to power agricultural machinery. When a tow hitch was fitted together with a rear PTO, an extension plate was needed to provide clearance.

Power take-offs were a vital element, and this November 1949 sales leaflet illustrated and promoted the centre PTO.

Stripped for action! This restored 1949 model in the later Bronze Green colour shows the original 'lights-behind' grille and the 'spade' type of seat backs.

Larger headlights on this 1951 model are framed by a different grille.

The dashboard was both functional and neat. This restored example in Australia shows the small forest of gear selector levers associated with the later 80s.

Hardtops were normally painted cream, but this one matched the Post Office Telephones livery on the rest of the Land-Rover. Clear here is the lift-up 'cat flap' above the tailgate.

This February 1950 sales catalogue shows the Land-Rover literally on top of the world. The implied message about its export success would not have been lost at the time.

It therefore made sense to carry on using this colour for civilian models as well. A subsidiary reason for the change may have been that the light 'No 2' green was about to be discontinued on Rover saloons, and so this was as good a time to make a change as any. The new colour certainly suited the Land-Rover.

Rover cars were still having an influence on Land-Rovers by the end of 1949. The P3 saloons went out of production in late summer and were replaced by the new P4 types, which had a revised gearbox. This gearbox, which had a taller third gear ratio, now became the sole type in production, and some time around the end of the year became standard for Land-Rovers as well. At the same time, the ring-pull freewheel control was changed for a lever with a yellow grip to distinguish it from the transfer box control, which had a red grip.

February 1950 brought the option of a hardtop for the body – a roof panel, two side sections and a hinged upper tailgate. This was usually painted cream to reduce interior temperatures. Two more visual changes followed. In February 1950, shovel-shaped seat backs replaced the 'spade' type standard since October 1948, and in May the front-end design changed. Larger 7in headlamps replaced the original 5in size, and with them came a new grille with circular cut-outs that framed them.

The last of the major changes to these original models with the 1.6-litre engine – which had not been available in Rover cars since autumn 1949 – occurred on the 1951 models that were introduced in October 1950. A selectable four-wheel-drive system replaced the original permanent four-wheel-drive system with freewheel. The new system allowed the drive to the front axle to be disconnected in High range, to the benefit of tyre wear, fuel economy and component life, but four-wheel drive was still permanently engaged in Low range. On Land-Rovers with the selectable system, the earlier freewheel control with its yellow grip was simply repurposed to engage or disengage the drive to the front axle.

The 1950 Land-Rovers were to be the last ones with the original 1.6-litre engine. Rover was already aware that its customers wanted better road performance, and to that end had experimented during 1950 with a trial batch of 50 engines bored out to give a 2-litre size. This engine would take over as the standard type for the 1951 model-year.

The 2-litre Models, 1951–53

The Land-Rover engine was enlarged to a nominal 2-litre size in the same 1950 programme that produced an experimental 2.6-litre engine for the P4 saloons (*see* Chapter 8). The cylinder bores were enlarged on their existing centres, which precluded the retention of a water jacket between each cylinder. They were therefore grouped in pairs – 'siamesed' – with a water jacket between each pair. On the car engines, this gave trouble, but on test the siamese-bore Land-Rover engine gave no trouble at all and was therefore signed off for production.

Land-Rovers therefore had the new 2-litre engine for the 1952 season that began in autumn 1951. Its extra 2bhp was of little consequence, but the 25 per cent increase in maximum torque made a big difference, especially because it was now generated at 1,500rpm instead of the 2,000rpm of the old engine. The 1952 models were visually distinguished by a simple inverted-T shaped radiator grille that left the headlamps exposed, and by car-type exterior door handles. The sidelights also moved from the bulkhead to the fronts of the wings to meet lighting regulations in some export territories. Less visible were changes to the chassis, which had been strengthened with two transverse bracings and outrigger supports.

Production was running at 400 vehicles a week by the end of January 1952 – an increase of 50 a week since June 1950. Expansion had certainly slowed down, but it was not for want of orders, which continued to exceed Solihull's ability to build the vehicles. Further expansion

THE WELDER AND THE TICKFORD STATION WAGON

It was standard Rover practice to allocate special chassis series to special models and to number them with a distinctive prefix. The company did so for the 1947 Twelve Tourers and the planned P3 Drophead Coupés, and followed the same pattern for its Land-Rovers.

The 1948 Amsterdam show Land-Rover was configured as a mobile welding plant, with its generator made by the Lincoln Electric Co Ltd and driven by belts from the centre PTO. Believing that this variant had a bright future, Rover made it a catalogued model in 1949, with its own chassis prefix of 868. However, sales were slow, and although the Welder remained available until 1953, it was then abandoned as a separate 'factory' model.

Also given its own chassis series was the station wagon variant, which had an 867 prefix for 1949. The first example (on pre-production chassis L20) was presented at the October 1948 Commercial Motor Show, with a special body by the coachbuilder Tickford, who had built drophead coupé bodies for Rover in the 1930s and had designed a new one for the P3 models (*see* Chapter 5). The station wagon body was built by traditional methods, with lightweight aluminium alloy panels on a wooden frame. The wood was mahogany, partly because it would withstand tropical conditions and partly because there was still a shortage of the coachbuilders' traditional seasoned ash after the war. There were seven seats, with three individual seats in the front and four inward-facing foldaway seats at the rear.

Maurice Wilks had seen the potential for a passenger-carrying Land-Rover in addition to the purely utility model. He had clearly also seen the big Jeep station wagon which had been announced in the USA in 1946 on a long-wheelbase chassis. This had an all-steel body that was pressed and painted to look like a traditional 'woody' station wagon, and the Tickford body for the Land-Rover had the same decorative pressings on its side panels. There was more American influence on his thinking, too: he called it a 'station wagon', using the American term rather than the more familiar British one of shooting brake.

Station wagons theoretically became available in December 1948 after a slightly modified second prototype had been built on a standard chassis, but in practice production did not begin until May 1949, and almost all the 1949 models were shipped abroad to meet export requirements. There was some production for the home market during the 1950 season, but a large proportion of that year's Tickfords went to the UNICEF charity, which used them in support of its work in Finland, Poland and Yugoslavia.

Demand for the station wagon generally was slow, and the main reason was cost: the basic cost of the vehicle was around 50 per cent more than that of a standard Land-Rover, thanks to its hand-made coachbuilt body. British buyers also had to pay purchase tax because the station wagon was a passenger-carrying vehicle. This raised its showroom price up to the same level as that of a quality saloon car. So it was no real surprise that Rover ended production of the model after the 1950 season; at a time when demand for the standard Land-Rover was beginning to outstrip the company's ability to build them, the Tickford was an expensive headache that was just not necessary to Rover's profitability.

A final batch of 100 was built in mid-1950, mostly to meet outstanding export orders, and these were sold as 1951 models – some of them apparently being given the new-style 1951-season front-end details. Just 650 examples of the Tickford station wagon had been made in three years, plus two prototypes. That strong demand for a passenger-carrying Land-Rover existed was proved beyond doubt when Rover developed a station wagon that could be built on the main assembly lines as a 1954 model: the problems with the Tickford had been cost and its inability to fit into the mainstream production process.

The Tickford Station Wagon was not a success in sales terms, but this carefully restored example shows what a handsome vehicle it was.

The Tickford had seats for seven: the inward-facing ones in the rear could be folded up to provide more carrying space.

A small ceremony for the 50,000th Land-Rover in 1952. It was a 2-litre model with the inverted-T grille, destined for the British army, and was painted in 'desert' colours rather than the standard Bronze Green. Standing by the left-hand front wing is Arthur Goddard.

of production would need more factory space and more capital, and the Board turned its attention to securing both during 1952.

Meanwhile, the 50,000th Land-Rover came off the lines on 15 January 1952. Export sales were affected by the closure of some markets to imported vehicles – including the formerly strong markets of Australia, New Zealand and Brazil – but eventually CKD assembly (*see* Appendix III) found a way around this and Land-Rover sales figures continued to rise. The gradual easing of supply difficulties that had constrained the early days of Land-Rover production made its own contribution, but the British government still emphasised the importance of exports, and Rover was still constrained by what were known as 'home quotas' – the numbers of vehicles it was allowed to sell on the home market.

All this resulted in 1953-season production totals of the basic Land-Rover falling by around 20 per cent, as compared to the previous season. Yet 1953 was a better year overall than 1952 for Land-Rover production, and that solely as a result of a massive increase in the export of LHD CKD kits. And in the meantime, Rover were working on the development of new models – the 86in and 107in Land-Rovers that would take over from the 80in types in autumn 1953 as 1954 models.

Production Changes, 1952–53

There were far fewer running changes to the 2-litre Land-Rovers than there had been to their 1.6-litre predecessors; most of the early problems had been eliminated and there was no need for constant improvements.

Making enough Land-Rovers to meet worldwide demand was a constant headache. This assembly-line picture dates from late 1951.

The 1952 season nevertheless brought a few changes. After about 6,000 vehicles had been built, there was yet another change to the seats, which gained squarer and flatter backs, with more padding than before. Then somewhere around March 1952, a 'window soft top' became available for export (with perspex windows in the sides of the tilt), but not in Britain. Like the window hardtop that had become available for export earlier, it would have incurred purchase tax by changing the Land-Rover from a commercial vehicle into a (potential) passenger-carrying type. A truck cab also became available from about June 1952, although possibly earlier for export. This consisted of a detachable aluminium roof and back panel that were normally painted cream to reduce heat absorption.

There were no major changes for the 1953 models, although a dynamo with a slightly higher output was introduced mid-season. Nevertheless, there was an interesting variation on small numbers of 1952 and 1953 models, which were built with a fabricated bulkhead in place of the standard pressed steel type. The reason has never been determined for certain, but the most likely explanation is that Rover maintained a small stock of fabricated bulkheads against the possibility of supply shortages, and that they needed to use some of these over the winters of 1951–52 and 1952–53.

Conversions and Adaptations

Maurice Wilks had always intended that the Land-Rover should be a flexible and adaptable

The LAND-ROVER

FITTED WITH TRUCK CAB

THE metal cab has been primarily designed for converting the Land-Rover into a small pick-up truck, when the Metal Detachable Top (E.7) would be an encumbrance to loading and discharging a vehicle principally engaged in light transport operations. This type of cab may also be fitted when it is desired to give to the driving compartment, a more weatherproof protection than that offered by the canvas hood.

More accessories, and this time it was the Truck Cab. This sales leaflet was issued in June 1952.

THE FIRE ENGINE

Rover's experience with the Land-Rover fire engine was in many ways similar to its experience with the welder and station wagon models. Again probably taking their cue from Willys (who had developed a Fire Jeep from their post-war civilian CJ-2A model), Rover were experimenting with a Land-Rover fire engine by September 1948, again basing the prototype on a pre-production vehicle, R06. The aim was to create a small rural or factory fire-fighting vehicle.

It would be 1951 before a production model became available, probably because the company was simply too busy building the mainstream models to concentrate on its development. Meanwhile, several fire brigades had seen the Land-Rover's potential and had made their own adaptations. The earliest known was done in Portugal in 1948, and the earliest known in Britain was a batch of four owned by the Derbyshire Fire Service in 1949.

Land-Rover developed a standardised design, but oddly did not allocate a separate chassis number series for it. The company also quickly came to realise that individual fire brigades wanted features to suit their own needs, and that meeting these simply led to complications and production delays. The Land-Rover fire engine remained available beyond the 1953 cut-off point of this book, but Rover handed responsibility for its multiple variations to the technical service department in 1955. Later still, fire engine adaptations were left to specialist companies, to relieve Rover of the complications involved.

Probably the earliest adaptation of the Land-Rover as a fire tender outside the factory was this 1948 model in Portugal.

Dating from May 1953, this sales brochure was for the Land-Rover Fire Engine.

Another early fire service adaptation was this one by the Derbyshire brigade, which carried neither pump nor ladder but was nevertheless a useful support vehicle.

THE
LAND-ROVER
FIRE ENGINE

PRICE	£905	0	0
METAL DETACHABLE CAB available as an optional extra	£25	11	0

ALL VEHICLES ARE SOLD SUBJECT TO PRICE CURRENT AT TIME OF DELIVERY.

MAY, 1953

As with the cars, so with the Land-Rovers: the price insert for sales literature was a small one that could be changed if prices changed, without the need to alter the more expensive brochure.

OVERSEAS ASSEMBLY

The Land-Rover overseas assembly operations are discussed in Appendix III, and in some cases led to quite major variations from the standard specification.

In Belgium, Minerva constructed 80-inch models for the Gendarmerie and the army, adding their own steel bodywork with distinctive sloping front wings. In West Germany, the Bundesgrenzschutz (BGS, or Federal Border Police) also had steel-bodied vehicles, in this case built to meet their requirements on part-assembled chassis shipped to Vidal & Sohn in Hamburg.

The first Minerva models were built on 1952 chassis. This restored example originally belonged to the Gendarmerie, and shows the Minerva's unique sloping front wings.

The steel bodies of the Tempo vehicles for the BGS were also quite special. Note the locker on the bonnet (where the sidescreens could be stored), the tall doors with external handles, and the lidded lockers built into the front wings.

The Minervas were not all built up immediately on arrival in Belgium, and many were stockpiled until needed. This identification plate is for a 1953 chassis that was not built up until 1954.

Tempo seats were also quite different from the standard type, and tilted forwards to give access to the rear.

platform, and introduced a number of extras for it. However, the Land-Rover's popularity with farmers soon prompted specialist farm equipment suppliers to take an interest as well, and some of the earliest conversions came from such companies. At this stage of the Land-Rover's existence – and for some years after the 1953 cut-off for this book – these aftermarket conversions were not subject to any form of regulation, and the specialist converters could produce more or less whatever they thought would sell.

Whether any of these conversions actually caused the failure of components on the Land-Rover is not clear, but Rover obviously thought the potential for such problems existed. The question then would be whether Rover would or would not honour its basic vehicle warranty. Later, the company followed the lead of tractor manufacturers who faced the same problem, and introduced an approval system. Under this system, Rover would test an aftermarket conversion or accessory (at its maker's expense). If it was found to present no threat to the longevity and operation of the basic vehicle, it would be awarded Land-Rover Approval and the factory warranty would be honoured in case of failure. If it did present a threat, Rover could obviously not prevent it from being sold, but the withdrawal of the factory warranty from any vehicle with an unapproved conversion would certainly have been an obstacle to the sales of that conversion.

As already explained, several early conversions were prototyped on pre-production Land-Rovers, and therefore of course at Rover's invitation.

A batch of Land-Rovers ordered by the British army was used to test the Rolls-Royce B40 engine intended for the Austin Champ. This 2.8-litre four-cylinder engine was physically much larger than the standard 1.6-litre, and a repositioned axle left the test vehicles with an 81-inch wheelbase.

There was the welder (by the Lincoln Electric Co) on L05; the fire tender (incorporating a Pegson pump) on R06; a crop sprayer (by Dorman) on R17; and the station wagon on L20 (by Tickford). By spring 1949, the purpose-designed Brockhouse trailer was on sale, and by December 1949 there was a mobile compressor (by Bullows).

Other agricultural tools began to appear early on. Whatley Brothers of Bucklebury offered a side cutter, driven (probably) from the centre PTO; E. Allman & Co of Chichester had a PTO-driven saw bench and by November 1951 another crop sprayer, called the Plantector. An Eezion 'kneeling' transporter conversion was prototyped, probably some time after 1952, although it would be many more years before this conversion entered the frame again.

Then there were opportunities to fill the gaps that Rover had created. The company made inward-facing rear seats available for military Land-Rovers from 1949, but did not offer them on the civilian market because they would have turned the vehicle into a passenger carrier and therefore made it subject to purchase tax. (They became available for export in March 1951.) That did not stop some customers in Britain wanting them, and to meet demand a Leeds coach-trimming company, J. & L. White, made a set available to their own design.

The high cost of the Tickford station wagon and its demise in 1951 prompted several aftermarket confections, although it is likely that all remained one-offs. Within Rover, workshop foreman Ralph Nash had Abbey Panels of Coventry build him a special body on the chassis of R02 in 1949, which he had bought from the company. Commercial bodybuilders Perkins Longton in Staffordshire built a reasonable facsimile of the Tickford body on a June 1949 chassis, although it is not clear when they did so. Garage door specialists Ernest Battley of Coventry built a window hardtop on a 1952 chassis (although the exact date of manufacture is unknown), and in approximately 1952, Kiitokori Oy in Finland built at least one station wagon body on a Land-Rover chassis.

SAMPLE PRICES FOR LAND-ROVERS, 1948–53

		Retail price	Purchase tax	Total
1948, Jun	Basic	£450	N/A	£450
1948, Oct	Basic	£540	N/A	£540
1949	Welder	£825	N/A	£825
1949, Sep	Station Wagon	£750	£209 1s 8d	£959 1s 8d
1952, Jan	Basic	£598	N/A	£598
1953, May	Fire Engine	£905	N/A	£905

In May 1953, a metal cab for the fire engine cost an extra £25 11s 0d.

CHASSIS NUMBERS AND PRODUCTION TOTALS, LAND-ROVER 80-INCH MODELS

The chassis numbers of Land-Rovers built between 1948 and 1950 were normally prefixed by R (for RHD) or L (for LHD) as appropriate.

Note that a dash is used here between the identifying type prefix and the serial number to aid clarity; it does not appear on the chassis plates themselves.

Season	*Type*	*Chassis sequence*	*Total*
1948	Basic	86-0001 to 86-3000	3,000
1949	Basic	866-3001 to 866-7920	4,920
	Station Wagon	867-0001 to 867-0070	70
	Welder	868-0001 to 868-0010	10
1950	Basic	0610-0001 to 0610-9999	9,999
	Basic	0611-0001 to 0611-5440	5,440
	Station Wagon	0620-0001 to 0620-0480	480
	Welder	0630-0001 to 0630-0030	30
	2-litre prototypes, RHD	0710-0001 to 0710-0050	50
1951	Basic, Home market	1610-0001 to 1610-3971	3,971
	Basic, LHD	1613-0001 to 1613-7601	7,601
	Basic, RHD export	1616-0001 to 1616-3268	3,268
	Station Wagon, LHD	1623-0001 to 1623-0080	80
	Station Wagon, RHD	1626-0001 to 1626-0020	20
	Welder, Home market	1630-0001 to 1630-0004	4
	Welder, LHD	1633-0001 to 1633-0007	7
	Welder, RHD export	1636-0001 to 1636-0009	9
	Basic, LHD, CKD	1663-0001 to 1663-0078	78
	Basic, RHD, CKD	1666-0001 to 1666-2320	2,320
1952	Basic, Home market	2610-0001 to 2610-5569	5,569
	Basic, LHD	2613-0001 to 2613-6424	6,424
	Basic, RHD export	2616-0001 to 2616-3614	3,614
	Welder, Home market	2630-0001 to 2630-0014	14
	Welder, LHD	2633-0001 to 2633-0013	13
	Welder, RHD export	2636-0001 to 2636-0004	4
	Basic, LHD, CKD	2663-0001 to 2663-1985	1,985
	Basic, RHD, CKD	2666-0001 to 2666-1092	1,092
1953	Basic, Home market	3610-0001 to 3610-4122	4,122
	Basic, LHD	3613-0001 to 3613-4613	4,613
	Basic, RHD export	3616-0001 to 3616-4007	4,007
	Welder, Home market	3630-0001 to 3630-0008	8
	Welder, LHD	3633-0001 to 3633-0007	7
	Welder, RHD export	3636-0001 to 3636-0007	7
	Basic, LHD, CKD	3663-0001 to 3663-7268	7,268
	Basic, RHD, CKD	3666-0001 to 3666-2240	2,240

Annual production (by model-year)

1948 3,000
1949 5,000
1950 15,999
1951 17,358
1952 18,715
1953 22,272

CHAPTER 8

A Thoroughly Modern Rover

The period between autumn 1946 and summer 1947 was a critical one for the Rover saloons as well as for the Land-Rover. After attempts to create a new saloon body style had run into the sand, as explained in Chapter 4, Maurice Wilks took the major decision to turn P3 into an interim model by adapting the pre-war body to suit the new engine and chassis that had already been designed. This would freshen the Rover range and help to maintain sales while work continued on the car that Wilks had originally intended, which would combine a modern body design with the new engine and chassis. That would be called P4.

This decision was vital because it gave Maurice Wilks more time to think, and it was during this period – probably in late 1946 – that he began to take a keen interest in the very latest in American car styling, as represented by the 1947 Studebakers. Actually announced in April 1946, these cars certainly were different from anything else at the time, although the rest of the US car industry soon copied their key features.

Most important was that the Studebakers had what we now call a three-box design, with a protruding boot visually balancing the bonnet; pre-war cars had mostly had sloping backs, and the current Rovers were fairly typical of the breed. The basic shape of the new Studebaker had come from industrial designer Raymond Loewy, had been tidied up for production by car stylist Virgil Exner, and was used on all the company's 1947 models. To Maurice Wilks, the most interesting one among them was the Studebaker Champion, which sat on a 112-inch wheelbase and was therefore closely similar in size to the current Rover saloons.

By summer 1947, Maurice Wilks had clearly persuaded his brother that this three-box styling was what Rover needed for the forthcoming P4 saloon. It certainly was ultra-modern (and this mattered because it would give Rover a design that would not date quickly), and it seemed to solve a number of problems at once. At the Rover Board meeting on 4 July, S. B. Wilks gave his fellow directors some insight into the latest thinking. He explained that the industry was moving towards wider and roomier bodies, which he said would involve taking the body out to the full width of the existing running boards. If the Board approved the new direction, it would need to approve the purchase of new dies that would cost in the region of £300,000. His mention of that figure may well have come from preliminary soundings with body manufacturer Pressed Steel. The designation of P4 was already in place,

The inspiration for the P4 body design was the 1947-model Studebaker Champion. This is one of the two that Rover bought to examine, pictured on Anglesey when a team from the Gas Turbine Department went to do some work on S. B. Wilks' boat, Torquil.

This rear view of a preserved car in New Zealand shows more of the features that would influence the P4 design.

and appears on a May 1947 specification document for the new model's rear axle produced by the Rover drawing office.

With the ground now carefully prepared, Maurice Wilks decided that he wanted a closer look at the Champion. There would not have been any of these cars in Britain at the time, as imports of foreign cars were forbidden in an attempt to help the re-emerging British motor industry, and so he clearly obtained special dispensation to order two of them direct from Studebaker. The identity of one of them is known from Rover's record of its sale to Henlys in London in 1951. It was on chassis G305131, came off the assembly lines at South Bend, Indiana on 19 September 1947, and was shipped to 'London, England' later that month. It probably reached Solihull some time around December, together with the second, unidentified, car. G305131 was painted in a colour called Alleghany Gray Light.

Neither of them seems to have been registered by Rover, and both probably always ran on trade plates while they were in use by the engineering department. One was dismantled and weighed, and no doubt Maurice Wilks' engineers pored over it. The other immediately went out on test.

Probably not much more happened on the P4 project in the later months of 1947, because Maurice Wilks and most of the Rover drawing office were working flat-out on the design of the Land-Rover while the Rover engineers were making the final adjustments to the P3 saloons before they entered production. Nevertheless, this may well have been the time when Maurice Wilks set about adapting the three-box styling to Rover's needs. He had his model-makers build three scale models to explore variations on the theme, which carried 'registrations' ROV 500, 501 and 502. The '50' number in each one probably indicated that he saw them as potential 1950 models. The shape was not quite there yet, but it was recognisably that of the eventual production P4.

ROV 500 was one of three scale models made to try out styling ideas for the P4. The influence of the Studebaker is obvious.

The sweeping line of the production rear end was already in place on the second model, ROV 501.

The bright metal lower body finisher on ROV 502 was another feature carried over to production.

Chassis and Drivetrain

Meanwhile, work had been going ahead on the engineering specification of the new saloon. There was probably never any doubt that it would have further-developed versions of the components destined for P3, with a box-section chassis frame, independent front suspension and the latest IOE engines.

Gordon Bashford's notebooks show a series of tests on the chassis from spring 1947 onwards, and the results of these tests probably also had an influence on the truncated P3 version. Six different experimental chassis were tested for torsional strength, and the sequence of tests suggests that Bashford was concerned with getting the maximum stiffness for the minimum weight.

It was probably late 1947 or early 1948 when a satisfactory frame design was achieved. This was to be a conventional full-length type rather than a three-quarter frame, as used for the P3. By May 1948, Bashford was calculating weights for both a six-cylinder car and a four-cylinder model, which suggests that the plan at this stage was to replace the P3 60 and 75 with comparable models of the P4. But over the next few months, it became clear that the new P4 was going to be very heavy. Both for this reason and because the unexpectedly high demand for the Land-Rover meant that there would not be enough four-cylinder engines for the saloon as well, further P4 development focused only on the six-cylinder model.

Even the six-cylinder engine in its existing P3 form with a single Solex carburettor was marginal with only 72bhp to haul the projected weight of the P4. During 1948, we know that Jack Swaine looked into using multiple carburettors, and at least one six-cylinder P3 was fitted experimentally with a triple-carburettor set-up (*see* Chapter 5). However, a less complicated and less expensive twin-carburettor arrangement giving 75bhp turned out to deliver acceptable results, and had probably been agreed by summer 1948, when the first prototype P4 chassis was constructed.

Both Jack Swaine and Maurice Wilks probably had their misgivings about the twin carburettors, as both men thought they would present maintenance problems in some of the export markets where Rover were now selling cars. This was probably why Swaine had started to look at a larger-capacity six-cylinder engine by late 1949, which would deliver more power but would need only a single carburettor. It later entered production for the Rover 90.

Not much needed to be done to the existing Rover gearbox to make it suitable for the P4, although the third gear ratio was altered to suit the characteristics of the twin-carburettor engine. The decision was also taken to raise the axle gearing from the 4.88:1 of the P3 to 4.7:1 for the P4. This was probably done to give the new model a higher top speed than the one it was to replace. As for the brakes, there was probably never any discussion about continuing with the hydro-mechanical system that had been introduced for the P3. Nevertheless, the front suspension was given longer bottom links and triangulated to absorb braking torque more effectively.

Body Design

In the meantime, Maurice Wilks had been refining his design for the P4 body. There was the interior to design as well as the exterior, and he seems to have called for ideas from instrument makers Smith's to provoke thought. American influence was very prominent here, and Wilks settled on a bench front seat (never before seen in a Rover) with a column gear change to allow room for a central third passenger. From the Studebaker came push-button interior door releases, which seemed very modern at the time. For the exterior, there seems to have been a 'first series' design, which the Rover directors inspected in February 1948 before agreeing that S. B. Wilks should obtain quotations for the necessary body dies. By the Board meeting of 26 April, the quotation was in at £230,000 – quite a lot less than the £300,000

Smith's Industries put forward some dashboard proposals. This one incorporates the rectangular instruments that would be a feature of the first P4s.

that the shrewd Wilks had suggested might be necessary at an earlier meeting. Unsurprisingly, nobody raised any objections.

All this design work took time, of course, and there was still no new body by the time that first full P4 prototype chassis was built in summer 1948. The P4 development team needed to get on with testing it as soon as they could, so somebody decided to fit it with the body of one of the two Studebaker Champions that the company had bought for evaluation: the two cars were very similar in size. The resulting 'mule' prototype was christened the Roverbaker, and Jack Swaine believed that the name was coined by C. A. 'Bro' Ward, who had been appointed to lead P4 development.

Gordon Bashford remembered taking the Roverbaker on its first long run to Torquay and back, in company with Roland Seale, the head of the Rover drawing office. 'The Studebaker body was an excellent disguise when used on public roads,' Jack Swaine remembered in 1980. Once its days as a test bed were over, the Roverbaker was rebuilt with its original Studebaker body and stylist Tony Poole remembered it becoming a general factory hack at Solihull. He believed that it was rebuilt at Rover with some non-Studebaker parts after a rear-end shunt, and then survived into the 1970s in the hands of a Rover employee.

Body and chassis development were so seriously out of phase with one another during 1948 that almost all the chassis work must have been done on the Roverbaker. The 'second series' full-size body mock-up was not completed until February 1949 – a good six months after the

The second-series full-size mock-up was pictured in February 1949 and, interestingly, had left-hand drive as well as the Viking nameplate. In the background are the overhead wires for the trolleybuses that used to run workmen's services into the factory at Solihull.

Roverbaker had gone on test. Interestingly, this new mock-up carried a badge that named it as a Rover Viking, but if that name was ever seriously proposed it did not go any further.

This was very much the production design, with rear 'suicide' doors (the ROV 500 series of models had different proposals) and with the slatted radiator grille containing a single central fog lamp. The famous 'Cyclops eye', incidentally, seems to have been inspired by the centrally-positioned auxiliary lamp of the P3, although it is quite likely that pictures of the 1948 Tucker Torpedo had nudged Wilks in the same direction. (Some people have suggested Studebaker influence, but that company's 'bullet' motif did not appear until its 1950 models were announced in mid-1949.) Of particular interest is that it featured headlamps set within box-like structures – which harked back to those on Maurice Wilks' July 1945 scale model for his proposed new post-war car (*see* Chapter 4).

This second-series mock-up was translated into a first prototype body in spring 1949. A second chassis had already been built and had been waiting for it since at least 5 April, when Gordon Bashford took some measurements from it and recorded them in his notebook. Its front suspension presumably incorporated the modifications made around January 1949 on P3 production when a problem with wheel shimmy had developed.

At long last, body and chassis now came together as the first full P4 prototype or 'first experimental car' as the photographic ledger calls it. It was photographed on either 3 May or 3 June 1949; infuriatingly, the handwritten photographic list is not clear. Nevertheless, this is almost certainly the white RHD car photographed in the factory

The first full prototype was pictured in May or June 1949. Note the bright finishers around the air intake grilles and headlights. Both features made production, but did not last long.

This must be the first production chassis, which was pictured in August 1949. The box-section frame was immensely strong, but also heavy.

grounds with a suited driver at the wheel. Whether it was numbered as P4/1 or as P4/2 (the Roverbaker perhaps having been P4/1) is unfortunately not clear.

The completion of this prototype was important progress – but it was also desperately, almost comically, close to the planned introduction of the new model in September and certainly too late for any major changes to be made. A few details were in fact tidied up, perhaps purely to simplify manufacture, but this was the car that was announced at the 1949 Earl's Court motor show as the new Rover 75.

The front suspension was a redesigned version of the P3 type, with much stronger lower wishbones.

The Early Cars

Exactly when P4 production began is hard to pin down. We know from the photographic archives that the first production chassis was finished on 17 August 1949, but it is clear that no completed cars were passed from production to despatch until 19 September. So it would be reasonable to suppose that Pressed Steel supplied the first bodies some time towards the middle of September, and that the assembly lines started rolling shortly afterwards.

Top priority must have been to get cars ready in time for the Earl's Court motor show in London at the end of September. No doubt it was something of a scramble to get five cars (one in each of the launch colours) plus a bare chassis together. Rover managed to get the second production car (0430-0002, JNX 124) into the Lord Mayor's parade that month as well, and this may have had to double as the pastel blue example on a revolving turntable at Earl's Court.

Production was very slow to get underway. In its first week, from 19 to 23 September, just ten cars were passed into the despatch department. The following week saw four more, and then there were no more for ten days. October was even slower. Cars were delivered in penny numbers to the despatch department, with large

The bench front seat was a new feature for a Rover, and again followed the lead of the Studebaker.

The rectangular instruments on the 1950 models did not go down well with buyers.

Push-button interior door handles were another borrowing from the Studebaker, and were another feature that was not much liked.

The six-cylinder engine was a twin-carburettor derivative of the one pioneered in the P3.

gaps between deliveries, and just twelve cars – two fewer than in September – were completed.

Clearly, there were difficulties, although it is not now possible to determine how much slow supplies from component makers played a part: such problems were a regular feature of car manufacturing as the industry struggled with shortages in the years after the war. Other issues probably arose because Rover had been developing the cars right up to the last minute, and Tony Poole, who was then a fitter in the gas turbine department, remembered that the first ones were assembled without holes in the bodywork for the starting-handle to pass through. The big gap in deliveries from production to despatch that occurred at the end of September and start of October suggests that this was a period of consolidation, when problems encountered on the first cars were being solved and plans were being made for a smooth start to volume production.

Volume production can be said to have begun in November. There was a regular flow of cars from production to despatch through the month, although quantities varied between one and seven a day, and there was a brief hiatus of two days (15–16 November) when no cars were delivered, and another on the last day of the month. A total of 46 cars were delivered to despatch in November, and then production began to reach sensible levels in December. By the end of the year, between 180 and 185 cars had been built, although a small number had been held back by the production department, either as samples (perhaps for training purposes) or because they were in some way unsatisfactory. These cars were released to despatch in the early months of 1950. By mid-1950, the lines were turning out 150 cars a week.

Changes

There were multiple changes to the specification before the end of 1949 and into early 1950, and many of these went unrecorded in Rover service literature. The choke, bonnet release and foot well vent control knobs on the earliest cars had flat grips, but these were soon changed to more substantial curved ones. All the first cars had chromed headlamp surround panels and chromed frames for the air intake grilles, but the intake frames disappeared early on and the chromed surround panels had gone by about January 1950 (and were probably fitted only to the first 200 or so cars). There had certainly been some grumblings from the public about too much chrome giving the car a very American and un-Rover-like appearance, but these items may actually have been deleted to simplify production or reduce costs.

The first cars also had a chrome finisher rail on the facia, but this was deleted at 0430-0191 in January 1950, according to service literature. It was also in early 1950 that a one-piece rear bumper replaced the original three-piece type; production difficulties may have been the main reason, because from an accident repair point of view the three-piece type made better sense.

The horn mounting was next to change, moving from under the bonnet (where the horns were muffled) to a very vulnerable position behind the front number-plate. The horns were given their own fuse box at the same time, although this was found unnecessary and was deleted shortly afterwards. The front wheel cylinders and brake

Pastel Blue was a favourite colour for the early 75. This car has the revised grille with just eight horizontal bars.

The Cyclops models had a distinctive boot handle above the number plate. The red reflectors were added after they became obligatory under new regulations in 1954.

shoes were then redesigned in February, and that same month brought modified rear lamp bodies and modified door check straps. In March (at 0430-1211) it was the turn of the handbrake, which had originally been a straight vertical rod but was now given a rearward extension that created the 'shepherd's crook' style.

April's changes were limited to a repositioned stop lamp switch and carburettors with a shorter suction chamber, and in June the stabiliser bracket on the rear axle casing was modified after giving trouble. But June also brought another and more major change. By the spring of 1950, overheating had become a problem. As a first step, the larger-capacity export-specification radiator was standardised on all models. Service literature for June 1950 says that the original 15-bar grille had now been changed on production to one that had only eight bars, and dealers were advised to remove alternate bars from the grilles of earlier cars that had an overheating problem. (The problem did not go away entirely. By December 1950, export cars were being fitted with a four-bladed cooling fan instead of the original and wholly inadequate two-bladed type.)

Press Reactions to the New 75

Rover were well aware that the new P4 75 was not really ready for production at the time of its launch, and so they delayed the preparation of a press demonstrator for several months. When it arrived, in the early summer of 1950, it was a Pastel Blue car registered as JWD 386 on 1 May, with chassis number 0430-0355.

This was an inordinately long time to keep the press waiting, and in the meantime some trusted members of the weekly magazines had been given short test drives, probably to prevent them complaining too loudly. At the same time, the inevitable negative comments had been made by writers who had not tried the car. 'It is not a bit like the old Rover,' complained the motoring correspondent of the *Bristol Evening World* on 29 September 1950; 'I don't like it.' Just a few days later, the *Birmingham Gazette* of 1 October reported that 'I have found very few motorists who approve of the new body styling.'

The Motor of 24 May 1950 contained the first proper road test, and summarised the 75 as

> *a car to which very great thought has been effectively applied, to details as well as to the major objectives of excellent handling, unusual refinement, a notable turn of speed and prolonged trouble-free life.*

The magazine acknowledged that its styling 'has offended some conservative tastes ... (but) is at least distinctive and functionally sound.'

The testers liked the smoothness and flexibility of the engine, but thought the car lacked sparkle in third and top gears and also commented negatively on the absence of synchromesh on second gear at a time when most other British cars had it. Despite soft springing, they found the car's handling stable and vice-free, although the steering was rather heavy at low speeds. They were not keen on the boot, which was adequately sized but suffered from having to contain the spare wheel. Nevertheless, 'in the matter of small details, this Rover reveals a quite unusual proportion of those minor points which make such a difference to pleasurable driving and ownership'.

The Autocar had published its views on the new 75 as early as September 1949, based on early runs in prototypes. At that stage, they had described it as:

> *... a superb car, beautifully suspended, accurate and light in steering, steady and stable on corners, deceptively lively because of its quietness, and possessed of one of the best steering column gear changes so far experienced. Altogether a car of superlative charm.*

Even so, when they published their test of JWD 386 in the issue of 14 July 1950, the testers made clear that the car had a lot to live up to.

They concluded that it did not disappoint, and 'with experience the feeling grows that a famous car has kept up with the times, both in exterior matters and in mechanical design'. They admired its stability and comfort, were politely scathing of the column gearchange, which 'is not so positive, like most of its kind,' and shared *The Motor*'s view that the new 75 had less acceleration in third and top gears than its P3 predecessor, as well as its criticism of the boot arrangements.

Beyond the specialist press, the car also quickly gained appreciation. In *Country Life* for 11 August 1950, John Eason Gibson wrote that:

> *I subjected it to a road test longer than normal in an effort to discover faults ... (and) ... not only was the car as smooth and silent at the end of this trip as at the beginning, but what is perhaps of even greater interest is that at the end of the test my impressions of the car were even more favourable than in the first few miles.*

The First 1951 Models

Those multiple adjustments to the P4's specification were not quite the end of the story, however. Rover was clearly not happy with the car yet, and for the 1951 models they prepared another set of changes. This time, their implementation was delayed by supply problems (still not at all uncommon in those days of post-war rationing) that resulted in a number of cars having a transitional specification. There were chassis numbering changes for 1951, too, as the export and CKD cars were given their own prefix numbers and numbering sequences. Home market cars were now prefixed with 1430.

The planned 1951 specification incorporated all-hydraulic brakes and a new high-pressure fuel pump that was relocated from under the bonnet to a chassis outrigger. The interior featured circular instruments (the rectangular ones had not been much liked), the clock was relocated in the centre of the facia rail where all passengers could see it, and the freewheel control moved from outboard of the steering wheel to inboard of it, alongside the heater controls. The positions of some switches were reshuffled, the change switch from side to head lights becoming a stalk on the steering column and the lighting

EXPORTS

All the 1950-model cars had chassis numbers that began with the prefix 0430. On export models, that prefix followed an L (for left-hand drive) or an R (for right-hand drive), although there seem to have been some inconsistencies in the practice.

Production of cars for export began early on, with L0430-0012 in September, but no cars were actually exported until early December. This may have reflected shipping difficulties, but equally it may have indicated that Rover were not prepared to let any examples of their new car out of the UK until they had sorted out initial teething troubles. Only a handful of cars actually left the UK before the end of December, and these went to Belgium, Denmark, Eire, France, Finland, Guernsey, Holland, Iceland, Sweden and Switzerland.

The first 75 exported to the USA was L0430-0641 in February 1950. Cars for North America had flashing turn signals, and the semaphore arms were blanked off. The rear light back plate contained two separate bulbs instead of one, but the glass lens was still all red. The authorities in some states declared the central fog lamp illegal, and to cater for these Rover provided the 75 with a special chromed plate over the grille aperture, with the number 75 cut out of it. North American cars also had a larger heater box as standard.

Some US states outlawed the 'Cyclops eye', and for them Rover provided a bright metal cover plate with the number 75 cut out of it.

For the 1951 season, the instrument panel was redesigned with round dials.

Cyclops models in full production at Solihull in August 1951.

By the time of this April 1951 sales brochure, colour was returning to Rover's publicity material.

The ROVER "75"

PRICE	£910 0. 0
PURCHASE TAX	£253 10. 7
TOTAL	£1,163 10. 7

ALL CARS ARE SOLD SUBJECT TO PRICE AND PURCHASE TAX CURRENT AT TIME OF DELIVERY

MARCH 20TH, 1951

Prices were carried on a separate slip, so that they could be easily reprinted without the need to replace the full sales brochure.

master switch moving to the main instrument panel beside the dials. The courtesy lights were also re-wired to operate independently of the sidelights, and it was probably at this stage that the original 'cat's eye' lenses for the headlamps were replaced by block-pattern lenses.

All the 1951 cars had those changes. However, the planned 1951 specification also replaced the push-button interior door handles with conventional types, and changed the push-button front seat release to a more accessible lever. These alterations did not come on-stream at the start of the 1951 model-year, but were added progressively over the last few months of 1950. Just to complicate matters, supplies of the new door release mechanisms arrived before supplies of the new handles – and so 1,120 cars built in October and November had a 'temporary' shorter handle, and dealers seem to have replaced these by the correct ones when cars went in for service. In all, there were 1,330 cars built with a 'transitional' specification that was a hybrid of the 1950 and 1951 types.

So it was that the full 1951 specification, by this time with rising hinges for the front doors and less ornate courtesy lamps in the rear pillars, was in place only a month before 1951 itself began.

COLOURS AND TRIMS, ROVER P4 75 MODELS, 1949–53

1950 season

Paint	*Trim*
Black	Green, Grey or Red
Connaught Green	Grey
Ivory	Green or Red
Lakeside Green	Green
Pastel Blue	Blue

1951 season

Paint	*Trim*
Black	Beige, Blue, Green, Grey or Red
Connaught Green	Green or Grey
Ivory	Green or Red
Lakeside Green	Green
Pastel Blue	Blue

1952 season

Paint	*Trim*
Black	Blue, Green, Grey, Red or Tan
Connaught Green	Green or Grey
Ivory	Green or Red
Lakeside Green	Green
Pastel Blue	Blue

1953 season

Paint	*Trim*
Black	Blue, Green, Grey, Red or Tan
Ivory	Green, Red or Tan
Light Grey	Blue, Green, Grey or Red
Pastel Blue	Blue
Sage Green	Green, Grey, Red or Tan

Two-tone options	
Dark Grey over Light Grey	Blue, Green, Grey or Red
Sage Green over Light Green	Green, Grey, Red or Tan

EVER ONWARD

During the 1950 season, Rover was also looking actively at further development of the P4 range. A batch of 30 prototypes was built with a more powerful 2.6-litre engine to improve performance. There were also two experimental drophead coupés (plus a third body that was built for the gas turbine car JET 1), and an experimental fixed-head coupé, all made by Salmons-Tickford.

Neither the coupés nor the gas turbine car progressed beyond the experimental stage, but the 2.6-litre engine did. After a redesign to give more water between the cylinder bores, it became the power unit of the Rover 90 in 1953.

Fortunately, the constant stream of specification changes that had afflicted the 1950 models was now a thing of the past, and production of the P4 finally settled down.

The 1952 Models

The original P4 models had been brought to market with what might be called undue haste, and Rover had spent the first few months of production sorting out teething troubles and dealing with feedback from customers. They had encountered customer doubts about their appearance; there had been overheating difficulties; and the cars were not as refined as Rover would have liked. All these problems were therefore tackled in a programme to develop a heavily revised P4 for the 1952 season.

The cars were not ready in time for the traditional start to the Rover season at motor show time in the autumn, although Rover's regular contract photographer, John Toft-Bate, photographed an early example in mid-June 1951; he then took a further set on 22 August. The reasons for the delay are not clear, but production of the 1951 models was allowed to continue until the end of the calendar year, and the new 1952 models did not start coming off the lines until January that year. Showroom sales began before the end of January, although the formal public launch was not until the Geneva motor show, which opened on 20 March 1952. For this, Rover prepared a special display chassis.

Far more work went into the 1952-model Rover 75 than met the eye when the cars were announced. In typical Rover fashion, all the new season's changes looked like evolution when in fact they were the results of a comprehensive redesign. The development engineer in charge of the whole thing was Chris Goode, who had taken over leadership of the P4 project from 'Bro' Ward.

All the public saw at first glance was a new front end with a reassuringly Rover-like grille. It was certainly more attractive than the rather odd front end of the earlier Cyclops models, which had prompted some rumblings of discontent

Cyclops models had a unique badge, and the model name of 75 was not displayed anywhere on the car.

With the 1952 front-end redesign came a return to the style of grille badge used on the P3 75.

Looking a little brighter than the real Lakeside Green on this promotional postcard, this 1952 model shows off its new front end design.

Just visible here above the bulkhead is the new air intake, which could be raised and lowered by a lever inside the car.

The rear end was redesigned, too, with a different style of boot handle. This is actually a 1953 75, with reflectors below the lights added to meet later regulations.

The 1952-season models had the spare wheel under the boot floor, leaving a much more useable boot space.

Although the car's colour was fanciful, the new front end made a splash on this March 1952 sales brochure.

from Rover's traditional customers. However, that was far from being the point of the exercise. In fact, there were two very practical reasons why Rover had redesigned the front end.

On the one hand, the original horizontally slatted grille with its central fog lamp restricted airflow to the radiator and contributed to over-heating in some circumstances. On the other, the twin air intakes mounted below the headlamps picked up not only the air they were designed to feed to the heating and ventilating system but also exhaust fumes when the early cars were standing in traffic.

The new Rover front end was a brilliant but simple piece of design, and *The Motor* of 19 March 1952 beautifully understated the position when it wrote of the 'distinct improvement in appearance' for the latest models. In place of the body-colour grille came an elegant new one with a chromed brass frame and narrow vertical slats. Both these slats and the central spine were also chromed, and there was a traditional triangular Rover badge at the top centre. Above it, at the very nose of the bonnet, was a quite prominent chromed Viking's head emblem. The new grille not only harked back to the respected earlier designs but also let through the necessary amounts of cooling air.

The basic shape of the wings remained unchanged, but the headlamps were now recessed directly and neatly into the wing fronts; Lucas 'tripod' types also replaced the earlier headlamps with block-pattern lenses. The twin intakes below the headlamps meanwhile disappeared in a complete revision of the whole heating and cooling system. The design solution was again simple. A hinged flap was placed at the base of the windscreen, cutting into the back of the bonnet, and ideally placed to take in air at a level high enough to avoid exhaust fumes. It could be closed manually by a lever inside the car to prevent an excess of cold air getting into the cabin, and for good measure, a larger heater provided an increased output of $3\frac{1}{2}$ kilowatts.

The only casualty of this front-end redesign was that there was no longer a fog lamp as standard. Rover nevertheless compensated by offering one as an optional extra. It bolted to the neat new valance panel that filled the gap between the bodywork and the front bumper.

Surprisingly little information is available about the creation of this new front end. There can be no doubt that the driving force behind it was Rover's chief engineer, Maurice Wilks. He would certainly have been helped by Ben Loker, the chief body designer. But the inspiration behind it is not at all clear, and it is hard to find any obvious precedents. At the time when it must have been designed in 1951, American grilles tended to be horizontal, and European ones to be vertical. The exceptions were from some of the bespoke coachbuilders, primarily in France and in Italy.

The engine and gearbox of the 1952 chassis were essentially unchanged. The 75 still had its 2103cc six-cylinder IOE engine with twin SU carburettors, and the gearbox was still a four-speed with synchromesh only on third and top, a column-mounted change lever, and a freewheel. A new exhaust heat shield made a welcome reduction to the heat transmitted to the interior of the car, but the major improvement to the 1952 models' refinement came from new composite rubber and steel mountings between body and chassis that reduced the transmission of road noise into the bodyshell. Many years later, Spen King (who was working on gas turbines at the time) expressed his opinion that these new mountings completely transformed the P4.

Silentbloc mountings that used the same principle were also fitted to the front suspension, where rubber between springs and suspension arms stopped road noise being transmitted up the springs. Meanwhile, the rear chassis cross-member was now slightly dished to accommodate a wedge-shaped fuel tank. This whole area had been redesigned to provide better accommodation for the spare wheel, which now sat under the boot floor. The wheel was accessible through its own hinged door, which could be locked by a pin operated from inside the boot.

The boot also had a spring-balanced lid now, instead of the temperamental self-locking prop on the earlier cars, and a neater handle than before. Without the spare wheel, its floor was unobstructed, although it still sloped towards the rear. Starting handle and wheel brace had been moved, too, and were now clipped to the inner wing under the bonnet and no longer awkwardly clipped to the boot floor. The right-hand rear corner of the boot became the new (and permanent) home for the electric fuel pump, where it suffered from neither vapour locks (as on the 1950 cars) nor water damage (as on the 1951 models). A neat box-like cover trimmed in black leather cloth protected it from items stowed in the boot.

Invisibly, the body now sat an inch higher than before at the rear, giving extra passenger headroom. A wider rear window created a lighter interior, and better seat comfort came from a spring base underneath the cushions. The backrests for both seats were simplified, and no longer had separate side bolster panels, while a recessed back to the front one added knee room for rear passengers, and alterations lower down improved foot room.

The driver would have noticed a full circular horn ring instead of the half-ring of the earlier cars, while an organ-type accelerator pedal allowed more sensitive throttle control. On the facia, the glove-box handles now had recessed undersides, and new rotary switches replaced the earlier push-pull type. Instead of a low-fuel warning light, a switch gave access to a reserve supply of petrol (made possible by rearranged fuel lines and a solenoid changeover valve).

There were differently shaped locking handles for the front quarter-lights, and a major improvement was the addition of self-parking wipers. As the motor was switched off, so the wipers 'saluted' in the upright position before dropping down to park off the screen on the scuttle. Each wiper arm carried a small roller, which contacted a ramp on the lower beading of the screen frame to lift the whole assembly over the frame and park neatly below it.

Finally, Lucas had provided a number of improved electrical items for the 1952 models. Only the latest PF700 headlamps with their tripod support for the bulb hoods were immediately visible, but out of sight there were also a new distributor, a new dynamo with a greater output, and a new high-voltage coil that improved the engine's slow running.

Amid all this change, Rover chose not to offer any new paint or interior trim colours for 1952. So that season's models had the same five paint options and the same five leather options as before. Perhaps this was for manufacturing convenience, or perhaps it provided the sort of reassuring continuity that Rover customers seem to have liked. One further small change involving the paint was made, though: the rear light plinths, originally chromed, were now painted in the body colour.

THE 1952-SEASON ROVER GRILLE

The new grille design introduced for 1952 would remain in use on the P4 models until their production ended in 1964, albeit slightly modified over the years. A version of it would also be used on the P5 model introduced in 1958 and carried over with minor changes to the V8-engined P5B model that continued until 1973. So distinctive was the design that it was re-introduced on cars built by the Rover Group in 1991, slimmed down to suit the smaller frontal area of 1990s designs, but readily recognisable as a descendant of that original grille introduced nearly 40 years earlier.

The Rover grille was influential, too. In 1954, when commercial vehicle manufacturer AEC was looking for a more modern design to replace its traditional upright grille, its designers came up with one that had distinct similarities to the Rover design. It appeared on both trucks and buses – perhaps most famously on London's Routemaster bus – and remained in production until the end of the 1960s.

The 1952 Models in the Press

The new front-end appearance was welcomed by the UK motoring magazines. 'The net result has been to make the front look much more neat and also more distinctive,' said *The Autocar* of 21 March 1952, and *The Motor* later referred to 'a distinct improvement in appearance brought about by restyling the front'.

Both magazines tested the same 1952-model 75, registered LWD 787 on 27 February that year and on chassis number 2430-0459. *The Motor* published first, in its issue of 14 May, and after ten days and 1,800 miles with the car had finished with a great deal of respect for it. Their assessment perfectly encapsulated what the latest 75 was all about:

> *Intended to do a job of work as quietly and as efficiently as possible, the Rover is not the sort of car to arouse strongly partisan enthusiasms, for its very virtues call for application of the adjective 'unexciting'. The virtues, however, are very real and make the Rover 75 a car for which admiration slowly but very surely increases as substantial numbers of miles roll inconspicuously by.*

The Autocar test was published quite late, in the magazine's issue of 15 August. They bemoaned the lack of synchromesh on second gear, but found the car's road manners 'unusually good'. It was no sports car, but made an excellent touring machine and, they summarised, was:

> *...a comfortable, quiet and economical quality car that meets the requirements of many people who wish to get from place to place with a complete absence of fuss. It has a graceful exterior and tasteful interior, yet possesses a good measure of traditional character.*

The 1953 Models

The positive reception that greeted the 1952 models made clear that Rover did not need to make any major changes, and there were only small alterations for the 1953 season. The short strip of chrome trim on the scuttle vent flap was deleted and, early on, the chromed vertical grille slats gave way to slats with a duller, anodised finish. The reasons for both changes remain unknown, but neither seems to have prompted any public comment.

Nevertheless, there were some changes to the colour options. The Black, Ivory and Pastel Blue favourites were retained, but in place of the two greens came Sage Green and Light Grey. As for interior colours, the previous year's five options remained unchanged. Production of the 1953 models started in October 1952, but some of the last 1952 models, built in September and at the start of October, were also painted with 1953's new colours.

The basic five-colour paint range was also extended by extra-cost two-tone options, in which the roof was painted a darker colour than the lower body. The options featured the two new colours, but in each case with a second colour that was not available on its own. There was thus Dark Grey for the roof of Light Grey cars, while Light Green was used for the lower panels of cars with a Sage Green roof. Both combinations were most attractive, although the two-tone grey seems to have been more popular. Interestingly, several 1952 models had served as two-tone prototypes in the first half of the year, and rejected options included green with grey, and two-tone blue; Very Dark Red with red is also recorded, although this may have been an experimental single-tone paint with a red interior.

Just one major specification change was made during the 1953 season. It occurred quite early on, after just 1,238 cars had been made, and was the deletion of the Panhard rod on the rear axle. This had given some trouble on the earlier cars, and Rover had now concluded that it was unnecessary. They also suggested that dealers should remove it from older models when they came in for service, so few cars that survive still have it.

THE GETHIN'S FLOOR-CHANGE CONVERSION

Not every Rover buyer liked the column gear change of the early 75, and the Rover dealers at Tyseley – Gethin's – spotted an opportunity to offer a conversion. It is very likely that this was designed by Peter Wilks, who had of course designed the floor change for the 75 gearbox used in the Marauder but during 1952 had joined Gethin's as workshop manager. Wilks may well have proposed the conversion to his new employers, too.

The Gethin's sales leaflet claimed their conversion was:

> *...developed for many owners of the new Rover 75 who still prefer the original type of gear change. It retains all the pleasing characteristics of central change but the lever is offset towards the driver, permitting ample leg-room for the centre passenger.*

The conversion probably became available in late 1952 or 1953, and was still on offer as late as 1956, although it was never very common. It was available overseas as well, and there is evidence of a LHD car in the USA being fitted with one, suitably adapted. The main parts of the conversion were P3 items the main drawback being that the layout of the linkages required a back-to-front gate, with first and second gear to the right, and third and fourth on the left. Two versions were available, one using the standard P3 gear lever and the other with an extended gear lever that may have been intended to suit shorter drivers who found the P3 gear lever too far away. On the extended lever, the reverse button nevertheless remained at the junction of the main lever with the extension, which made use a little tricky.

Progress Quantified

As the 1952 season was just eight months long and the 1951 season lasted sixteen months, the actual production totals for these years can be misleading. However, combining the totals of 10,279 for 1951 and 5,768 for 1952 gives a figure of 16,047, and averaged out that gives just over 8,023 cars a year. That shows how much improvement had been made on the 1950-season figure of 5,250.

For the 1953 season, Rover probably deliberately capped production at 8,000 cars, leaving the major increase in the P4's popularity to come in the 1954 season when there were three models available rather than just one. And that year, the production total increased massively to 13,486, or more than 250 per cent of the first year's production total. Alongside the huge increases in demand for Land-Rovers, that made clear just how well Rover were now doing.

PRICES FOR THE P4 ROVERS, 1949–53

		Retail price	Purchase tax	Total
1949, Sep		£865	£241 0s 7d	£1,106 0s 7d
1951, Mar		£910	£253 10s 7d	£1,163 10s 7d
1951, Sep		£955	£532 1s 2d	£1,487 1s 2d

CHASSIS NUMBERS AND PRODUCTION TOTALS, ROVER P4 75 MODELS, 1949–53

Season	*Type*	*Chassis sequence*	*Total*
1950	Standard	0430-0001 to 0430-5220	5,220
	Experimental 2.6-litre	0530-0001 to 0530-0030	30
1951	Home market, RHD	1430-0001 to 1430-3211	3,211
	Export, LHD	1433-0001 to 1433-2718	2,718
	Export, RHD	1436-0001 to 1436-4921	4,921
	CKD, RHD	1466-0001 to 1466-0126	126
1952	Home Market, RHD	2430-0001 to 2430-1927	1,927
	Export, LHD	2433-0001 to 2433-2718	2,718
	Export, RHD	2436-0001 to 2436-0997	997
	CKD, LHD (*)	2463-0019 to 2463-0072	54
	CKD, RHD	2466-0001 to 2466-0054	54
1953	Home Market, RHD	3430-0001 to 3430-4742	4,742
	Export, LHD	3433-0001 to 3433-2036	2,036
	Export, RHD	3436-0001 to 3436-1068	1,068
	CKD, LHD	3463-0001 to 3463-0090	90
	CKD, RHD	3466-0001 to 3466-0064	64

(*) There is no surviving record of numbers 2463-0001 to 2463-0018, but it seems unlikely that they were not built. The eighteen cars would have made up three batches of the six typically associated with CKD shipping. The figures here and below assume that they were not built.

Annual Production (by Model-year)
1950 5,250
1951 10,976
1952 5,750
1953 8,000

CHAPTER 9

Where Next?

As Rover's sales began to rise and the company's financial position to stabilise at the start of the 1950s, those responsible for product development began to look ahead and to think of what might come next. For the Land-Rover, the version featuring the enlarged engine of 1951 would be followed by models with greater carrying capacity, and in the autumn of 1953 these entered production as the 86-inch and 107-inch models that replaced the original single 80-inch model. For Rover cars, the single-model range would be expanded to three models, as a version of the Land-Rover's new engine created the 60 and an enlarged six-cylinder created the 90 alongside the original 75 in autumn 1953.

These, though, were what might be called natural or even logical developments of existing products. Alongside them, Maurice Wilks' enthusiasm prompted some serious investigations into new products that, for one reason or another, never reached production. There was a scheme to develop a convertible derivative of the P4 saloons that might sit alongside the mainstream models in the same way that the elegant Tickford drophead coupés had accompanied the saloons and sports saloons of the late 1930s. There were plans for a fixed-head coupé as well. A good deal of work went into creating a hybrid of car and Land-Rover that was known from early on as the Road-Rover. And Maurice Wilks put a lot of thought into a less expensive, higher-volume car that might be introduced alongside the P4.

The Road-Rover

The timing of the Road-Rover idea strongly suggests that it arose from the ashes of the Tickford station wagon variant of the Land-Rover. As Chapter 7 explains, the cost of the Tickford's coachbuilt body made it far too expensive to sell, and so it was withdrawn. Yet Maurice Wilks seems to have been convinced that the basic concept of a rugged passenger-carrying model had merit.

It did not have to be based on a Land-Rover, but the P4 saloon chassis and running-gear would be sturdy enough for most likely buyers. Its cost could be kept down by making the bodywork as simple as possible. Buyers might be country-dwellers and farmer's wives who needed a tough, versatile and fairly basically equipped form of transport. They would not need the Land-Rover's four-wheel drive, which added both cost and complication – and for those who did, Rover would in any case soon be able to offer a completely redesigned Land-Rover station wagon that would be less costly than the earlier model. The name of Road-Rover may not have entered the picture until early 1952, but it was certainly an accurate description of what Wilks had in mind.

No time seems to have been wasted in making a start on what must have seemed like a promising idea. Maurice Wilks turned to his chassis designer Gordon Bashford to put forward some design proposals and, as Bashford explained it many years later, 'the aim was to produce a road car based to some extent on Land-Rover body structuring.' As early as September 1951 he drew up some layouts for what he called a 'Utility Car', but at this stage all kinds of schemes were under consideration. Some had Land-Rover bodies on P3 and P4 chassis frames, while others used new 'utility body' styles with Land-Rover or car chassis. Among the ideas were frameless construction (Bashford was then actively investigating chassis-less structures for future saloon cars) and front-wheel drive. There were even designs for a 'Land-Rover Staff Car on modified P4 chassis,' apparently for the army.

The decision to use a shortened P4 chassis had probably been taken by November 1951, when Bashford was working on the detail design of what he was still calling the Utility Car. Later documents show that a 97in wheelbase had been chosen (cut down from the P4's 111in size) and it is likely that this was settled some time in the last quarter of 1951, if not earlier. Certainly, some indication of the proposed size must have been settled before Maurice Wilks and his chief body designer, Ben Loker, started work on full-size mock-ups of the vehicle.

Surviving photographs of the mock-ups cannot be dated any more accurately than to 1951, but

This early wooden mock-up of the Road-Rover dates from late 1951 or 1952, and shows that a simple body design was always the intention. That EVC 301 number-plate had been used on several earlier mock-ups, notably for the P3.

The design had been slightly altered by the time of this mock-up, notably around the rear. The relationship between front wings and bonnet had also changed.

they make clear that Wilks was thinking in terms of flat panels wherever possible and a very simple, unadorned shape. It had one door on each side and sliding rather than winding windows to minimise build costs. The first version of the mock-up had a top-hinged window in the tail, but a further-developed version had a single rear door on the left and a fixed panel on the right. At the rear, both carried the EVC 301 number-plate that Wilks had used on the M Model and P3 mock-ups in 1945–46, and at the front they both had the dummy plate ROV 48.

By early 1952, work had started on a first prototype vehicle that became RR1 and was road-registered as MAC 162 in early April that year. No photographs showing it with that number-plate are known, but a few photographs that have come down through the Wilks family show what is almost certainly this vehicle, wearing trade plates 232 AC and standing outside S. B. Wilks' house at Street Ashton.

It certainly is crude in appearance – even more so than the mock-ups suggested – and Gordon Bashford remembered that it was 'nicknamed the "greenhouse" because of its slender framework and the amount of glass used.' A flat, one-piece windscreen went beyond the mock-up proposals, which had split windscreens. Records show that RR1 was built on the chassis of a P4 75 saloon, a 1952 RHD Export model numbered 2436-0500 – following the usual Rover practice of using Export chassis for anything out of the ordinary. Its engine was numbered RR1 and was probably a version of the 2.0-litre four-cylinder then in production for the Land-Rover.

Standard Rover practice at the time was to appoint a Project Engineer to co-ordinate work on projected new models, but no names of either

This picture, taken at S. B. Wilks' house in Street Ashton, shows what was probably the first Road-Rover prototype, running on trade plates. It is not hard to see why it gained the nickname of 'the greenhouse'!

Pictured at more or less the same spot, this is either the second or third Road-Rover. The body design is heavily influenced by Land-Rover practice.

Taken on the same occasion, this time looking towards the house, the vehicle shows a back body design that quite clearly anticipates the Land-Rover 86-inch station wagon of 1953.

a Road-Rover project engineer or the more junior members of his team have been discovered. Perhaps Maurice Wilks ran the project directly himself. What is clear is that good progress was made, and at least three more prototypes were built in 1952. Little is known about RR2, which ran on trade plates until becoming UWD 563 in 1956, but either this or RR3 (MWD 511) figures in some more remarkable pictures taken at Street Ashton House.

Reflecting the diversity of ideas that Gordon Bashford's early designs had incorporated, this second vehicle leans visually on the Land-Rover. Its roof panel, doors, side-opening tail door and two-piece windscreen with a galvanised frame are all Land-Rover in inspiration, if not actually in origin. Perhaps the body on the first prototype had proved as flimsy as it looked, and borrowing Land-Rover elements was a way of adding strength. It was an idea that was not pursued, though. The next design of Road-Rover body, as exemplified by RR4 (MWD 716) had much more in common with the full-size mock-up proposals of late 1951.

By this stage, a versatile seating arrangement for seven passengers was in place. There was room for three in the front, with a single seat for the driver and a bench seat for two passengers alongside, and behind these were three individual seats, all with folding backrests. There was an inward-facing jump seat behind them on the left-hand side, ahead of the single rear door, and the spare wheel was carried inside the fixed tail panel on the right-hand side.

The Road-Rover project had received acknowledgement from the Rover Board on 20 May 1952, when S. B. Wilks had included it in his presentation of plans for the company's future expansion. At this stage, he stated that £30,000 would be needed for development purposes, and that money presumably funded the first four prototypes and perhaps the five more that would be built during 1953. The design was not yet set in stone, and during January 1953, front-wheel drive again came under consideration, as did a

By the time of RR4, the body design had settled down. The door handles were still Land-Rover types.

This is probably RR4 again, with a seven-seat configuration. The spare wheel is mounted inside the body, on the right of the back panel.

By the time of RR9, the spare wheel had been moved to the outside of the back panel to give more space inside…

… but there appear to have been fewer seats and more room for items to be carried.

(hypothetical) 2.25-litre version of the V6 engine with which Jack Swaine's engine designers were experimenting.

No doubt these ideas were kicked into touch when S. B. Wilks formally proposed to the Rover Board on 15 April that the Road-Rover should be adopted for production. The Board agreed, and allotted a further £60,000 for the purchase of the necessary jigs, dies and tools. No production date was mentioned at this stage, but it seems probable that everybody now knew where the Road-Rover was going. All the prototypes since RR3 (and possibly RR2 as well) in late 1952 had the latest Spread-Bore version of the 2-litre engine (which would enter production in 1953), and such pictures as exist confirm that there had been no major changes to the body design.

Then at the Board meeting on 23 July, Road-Rover production was postponed. No reason was given, but in view of Rover's commitment to deliver two new Land-Rovers and two new variants of the P4 saloons that autumn, it is not hard to guess why postponement was considered necessary. The Board agreed that Road-Rover production would go ahead 'about June next year,' by which time presumably the pressure caused by the new-model introductions would have eased sufficiently.

The prototype programme continued throughout 1953. RR5 and RR6 had been completed in February and March, and RR7 followed in early July. The postponement of production must have given the project team an excuse to build more – and no doubt to incorporate further improvements – because RR8 followed in September and RR9 in November. There was then a pause in the build programme until June 1954, when RR10 was registered for the road.

It is not at all clear why Rover needed all these prototypes that appear from photographs to be essentially similar. Perhaps they did not really need them; perhaps they were built to give the development team something to do while the Board made up its mind about the Road-Rover's future. Gordon Bashford meanwhile used the

RR12 still survives, in the museum collection at Gaydon. This was the last gasp of the first-series Road Rover.

In this case, the rear door had been enlarged and centralised to improve access.

The instruments and steering wheel on RR12 reflected its links to Rover cars of the time.

time to look at front-wheel drive again, and by the end of May he was sketching up front suspension details for such an installation in the Road-Rover.

Looking perhaps further into the future, during July he was drawing up a whole series of further schemes. In addition to front-wheel drive, four-wheel drive had come into the picture, and there was some possibility that the vehicle might be offered in three different versions, with rear-wheel, front-wheel *and* four-wheel drive! Some consideration was also being given to a three-speed gearbox, double-reduction axles for the front-wheel drive and four-wheel drive versions, a double-wishbone independent front suspension with inboard brakes, a magnetic or friction clutch and, on the rear-wheel drive version, disc brakes.

It seems highly unlikely that any of this was more than theoretical, and the sheer variety of different ideas does rather suggest that the project had now lost its way. It hardly needs to be said that June 1954 came and went without any further reference to the Road-Rover project at Rover Board meetings. The number of prototypes gradually increased to twelve, which must have been double the number that the project really needed.

Essentially, the Road-Rover project now meandered on until the matter of finance for the project was raised again at a Rover Board meeting in March 1955. It was probably not long afterwards that the whole Road-Rover project was shaken up, most notably with a completely new body shape that seems to have been inspired by American station wagon styling of the day. The story of the Series II Road Rover prototypes runs far beyond the period covered by this book, but it should surprise no-one that it once again suffered from a lack of clear direction, or that the whole Road-Rover episode finally petered out in 1959. It was certainly not one of Rover's finer moments.

THE ROAD-ROVER PROTOTYPES

This list covers only prototypes built to the original design in the period 1952–55. There were eleven more Series II prototypes, built between 1956 and 1959.

Car number	*Engine number*	*Registration no.*	*Registration date*
RR1	RR1	MAC 162	08 April 1952
RR2	5713-1127	UWD 563	23 August 1956
RR3	SB2/8	MWD 711	17 December 1952
RR4	SB2/7	MWD 716	24 December 1952
RR5	SB2/11	NAC 214	13 February 1953
RR6	SB2/12	NAC 930	31 March 1953
RR7	SB2/17	NUE 665	09 July 1953
RR8	SB2/15	NWD 522	17 September 1953
RR9	SB2/9	OAC 816	30 November 1953
RR10	SB2/28	PNX 407	29 June 1954
RR11	SB2/29	PUE 41	28 July 1954
RR12	SB2/35	SNX 36	09 June 1955

Notes:
RR2: The original engine number for this prototype is not known. The one listed was a replacement that was probably fitted in 1956, when the car passed to a Rover employee and was road-registered for the first time.
RR5: The registration date for this one is actually recorded as 13 February 1952, which is clearly a mistake.
RR12: This is the only surviving prototype from this first group. It belongs to the BMIHT Collection at the British Motor Museum in Gaydon.

More Glamorous P4s

The appearance of a prototype P3 drophead coupé on the Rover stand at Earl's Court in 1948 made clear that the company was nursing ideas of adding such a car to the range as soon as economic conditions permitted. It had even turned for the coachbuilt bodywork to Salmons & Sons, now trading as Tickford, who had built the delightful drophead coupés for Rover chassis in the years immediately preceding the war.

The relationship with Tickford was still strong. Rover turned to that company for two more projects in the late 1940s, one being the Land-Rover Station Wagon that was announced in 1948, and the second being the special body for the gas turbine car JET 1 that was based on the shape of the P4 saloons that were new in 1949.

The Tickford Prototypes

The sleek two-door body for JET 1 was a great success, and there can be little doubt that it revived Maurice Wilks' enthusiasm for a new Rover drophead coupé. It was probably not long after JET 1 was revealed to the public in March 1950 that he asked Tickford to design and build a three-position drophead coupé body for the P4, using the lines of JET 1 as far as possible. For good measure, he also asked for a fixed-head version of the same design.

Tickford's first prototype was a black drophead coupé on chassis 0430-1279, which probably dated from around March 1950. The converted car was back at Solihull by early August, when it was photographed. It was stunningly attractive – and it certainly attracted the attention of the local Solihull MP, Sir Martin Lindsay. To cut

Inspired by the gas turbine car JET 1, the Tickford-converted P4 was an elegant-looking machine. This one was passed to Rover's local MP.

The other Tickford P4 drophead was finished in Pastel Blue, which always looked good with the P4 shape. It has been painstakingly restored from a near-derelict.

The lines of the drophead body worked very well from the rear, too.

Tickford built just one fixed-head coupé, and this is one of only two known pictures of it. Its three-piece rear window inspired the later P4 facelift.

a long story short, he persuaded Rover to sell it to him, which they did in late October after first registering it as KNX 518. Many years later, Sir Martin recalled paying £1,000 for it, which was something of a bargain when a standard P4 saloon cost just over £1,163! No doubt the knowledge that two more cars were on order from Tickford made Rover less reluctant to part with the car than they might otherwise have been.

It was probably in August that two more 75 saloons were pulled from the assembly lines and delivered to Tickford for that company to work its magic. One was to become a second drophead coupé, and the other was to become its fixed-head counterpart. The drophead, on chassis 0430-3707, was finished in Pastel Blue; the fixed-head, on chassis 0430-3709, was in a non-production light grey colour with a roof covering of rubberised canvas duck material that made it look like a drophead coupé from a distance. This car had a large, wrap-around rear window that was divided into three sections by vertical chromed strips and was undoubtedly the inspiration for the new rear window on the 1955-model P4 saloons.

Rover retained these cars without registering them for the road, and presumably they were used on trade plates while being evaluated. However, by summer 1951, the company had clearly decided not to put them into production. Rover registered the fixed-head car as LAC 447 in May before selling it on to one of their major dealers, Henlys in London. The drophead became LOK 918 in July and was probably registered by Collier's of Birmingham, another major Rover dealer. Both cars were subsequently sold to customers, but only the drophead survives today; the fixed-head car was scrapped some time around 1970.

Exactly why the project was brought to an end is not clear, although one possibility is that the cancellation during 1951 of the contract for Land-Rover station wagon bodies from Tickford led to a situation where Rover did not feel they could negotiate another contract with the company. Another possibility is that Maurice Wilks believed it would be preferable to go for a more glamorous body design than could be achieved on the basis of the production saloon body – and his next move would certainly support that hypothesis.

The Pinin Farina Prototypes

By the early 1950s, Italian coachbuilders were setting the pace for stylistic innovation in the motoring world. One reason for this was that the cottage-industry nature of much of the Italian coachbuilding business enabled it to risk innovation at a time when major coachbuilders in Britain were focusing on conservative designs as their market contracted. Another was that the new Italian marque of Ferrari was producing exciting cars that were for the most part bodied in Italy and therefore served as a glamorous advertisement for Italian coachbuilding.

One of the rising stars in Italian coachbuilding during the late 1940s was Pinin Farina. The company had been founded in 1930 and had developed a reputation for innovation, but was relatively little known outside Italy. Post-war, some striking designs had gained it attention on the world stage, and in particular the company forged strong links with Lancia. Known after 1960 as Pininfarina (all one word), the company took its name from Battista Farina, who was the younger brother of the coachbuilder Giovanni Farina; Pinin is a Torinese dialect word meaning the youngest of the family.

Rover's chief engineer Maurice Wilks was already attracted to Lancia's advanced engineering – their V6 engine and rear transaxle fascinated him, and he had Rover buy a Lancia for examination early in 1953 – and it may well have been this that led him to look more closely at what Carrozzeria Pinin Farina was doing. He liked what he saw, and he probably reasoned that a glamorous body designed by a fashionable Italian coachbuilder would give Rover a valuable edge in the relatively limited market for drophead coupé models. The obvious competitor models from Armstrong-Siddeley, Riley and others were still resolutely pre-war in appearance, and would offer no serious competition.

By November 1951, he had made up his mind. Rover would commission Pinin Farina to build a prototype drophead coupé on the existing P4 chassis. A memo dated 22 November arranged for a right-hand-drive export 75 chassis to:

> *... be shipped to Messrs Pinin Farina of Italy, who will manufacture and mount on it a Body to their own design. The Car, when completed, will be returned to Solihull, for testing and despatch.*

The Pinin Farina drophead body was a stunning design that drew on shapes favoured by the coachbuilder at the time. Its wide grille inspired the later Rover P5 design.

The drophead prototype has been carefully restored in its original Satin Bronze colour.

The Pinin Farina fixed-head car was another outstanding design.

The fixed-head was converted to left-hand drive before being sold to Spain, where it was pictured.

The chassis was to be 'despatched in the condition in which it normally reaches the Body Mounting Point, plus Road Wheels and Steering Wheel, to enable it to be handled prior to packing,' and it would be packed with a number of additional loose items, including a radio set from the service department. Among the loose items would also be a number of sub-assemblies that would be bolted together, as Rover thought the necessary BSF bolts and nuts would be hard to obtain in Italy!

The chassis that left Solihull on 1 February 1952 was number 2436-0001, and was the first of the 1952-season right-hand-drive export types. HM Customs and Excise approved the shipping on 16 February, and the chassis then departed for Turin. Exactly when it returned to Solihull with its new body is not clear, but the very first photographs of it appear to have been taken in the summer of 1953, which was some eighteen months after the bare chassis had left Solihull. Of some interest is that they were taken by Rover's own new technical films department rather than by the company's regular contract photographer, John Toft-Bate – but this may reflect nothing more than an early stage in the handover of responsibilities between the two.

Part of Rover's strategy was clearly to use this car to draw attention to the new models that were to be introduced at the Earl's Court show in autumn 1953. Its appearance on the show stand alongside the new 60 and 90 and the revised 75 certainly did that. Painted in Satin Bronze, a shimmering metallic gold, and upholstered in beige with a deep red convertible top and hood bag, it attracted a great deal of attention. Sleek and beautifully proportioned, it was 12 inches longer than a P4 saloon thanks to increased front and rear overhangs. It also featured a wide, recessed version of the latest Rover grille and a painted metal dashboard rather than the traditional Rover wooden type.

In its show review of 21 October 1953, *The Motor* described it as 'beautifully-proportioned', with 'unmistakable Rover characteristics ... blended perfectly with a body which combines dignity, elegance and practical comfort.' The magazine's staff were sufficiently impressed to give it a whole page description in that issue, and reported that Rover had already begun discussions about the manufacture of the drophead body in Britain.

No doubt they had, because in early 1954 Mulliner's of Bordesley Green started work on a 'production prototype' – a re-creation of the hand-built Pinin Farina car that adapted the design for low-volume manufacture and was built on a 1954-model 90 chassis (number 4530-0908). Its paint and trim were the same as the original. Meanwhile, Rover had also asked Pinin Farina to build a fixed-head coupé using the same lines, and that was built on a November 1953 RHD export chassis, number 4536-0261. This is thought to have been painted in metallic green.

By mid-1954, it appeared that Maurice Wilks' dream of P4-based drophead and fixed-head coupés was coming true, but two things caused its sudden demise. One was that Bertie Henly, who owned the big London Rover distributors and was a greatly respected figure in the motor industry, told S. B. Wilks that he was not prepared to sell a Rover drophead of any kind because he believed that drophead bodies would never be free of rattles. The other was that in June 1954 Mulliner's signed an agreement with Standard-Triumph to work exclusively for them after existing commitments to other customers were fulfilled.

So the cars were sold off. The original drophead went to Rover dealer Bill Apperley at New Brighton, near Wallasey, for his personal use, and was registered as OGX 576 (it was later re-registered as NHF 800). The Mulliner copy went to a Harley Street specialist who was married to Bertie Henly's daughter (and was the source of the story about Henly's dislike of dropheads). It became RNX 10 in January 1955. The fixed-head coupé remained at Solihull until October 1958, when it was registered as 2082 AC and sold to Senor Tabanera of Tabanera Romagosa, Rover's Spanish importers.

THE MYSTERY COUPÉ

S. B. Wilks told his fellow directors at the Rover Board meeting of 20 May 1952 that 'we are developing a two-door coupé from the P4 body panels, but we cannot yet say when or if this will go into production.' This was clearly not the Tickford conversion, which had been abandoned during 1951, and nor was it the Pinin Farina project, which did not use P4 body panels.

Tony Poole, who was then a fitter in the Gas Turbine Department, remembered a 'short, round-backed coupé' at about this time, which he believed was based on the P4, and which Maurice Wilks used a lot. The best candidate for this is recorded as EXPC/1 (Experimental Coupé, no.1?), which was registered as NWD 228 on 10 August 1952, and had a prototype 2-litre spread-bore engine (number SB2/7). It was later booked out to three Rover employees in succession, the last one having taken charge of it as late as June 1962. Unfortunately, its eventual fate is not recorded.

If Rover really did build a two-door P4-based coupé prototype at this time, the car must have been another dead-end in the saga of Maurice Wilks' attempts to develop a two-door model, which began with the Tickford cars in 1950–51 and ended with the Pinin Farina-styled cars of 1953–54.

There is little doubt that the Pinin Farina coupé had an influence on the design of the Rover 3-litre (P5) saloon that was being prepared in the mid-1950s, and its sale in the very month when the P5 was introduced seems to be further confirmation of that. Both the drophead cars survived at the time of writing but this one, sadly, has disappeared.

A New, Smaller Rover

The increased profits rolling in from Land-Rover sales encouraged the company's top management to think about adding a second car range alongside the P4. During late 1952, Maurice Wilks drew up an outline specification for this new car, which he called P5. He envisaged it as smaller than P4, and expected it to be built in larger volumes. It was to have a wheelbase of 103 inches, which would have made it about the same

Despite the registration plate of ROV 90, this appears to be one of David Bache's proposals for the new small Rover.

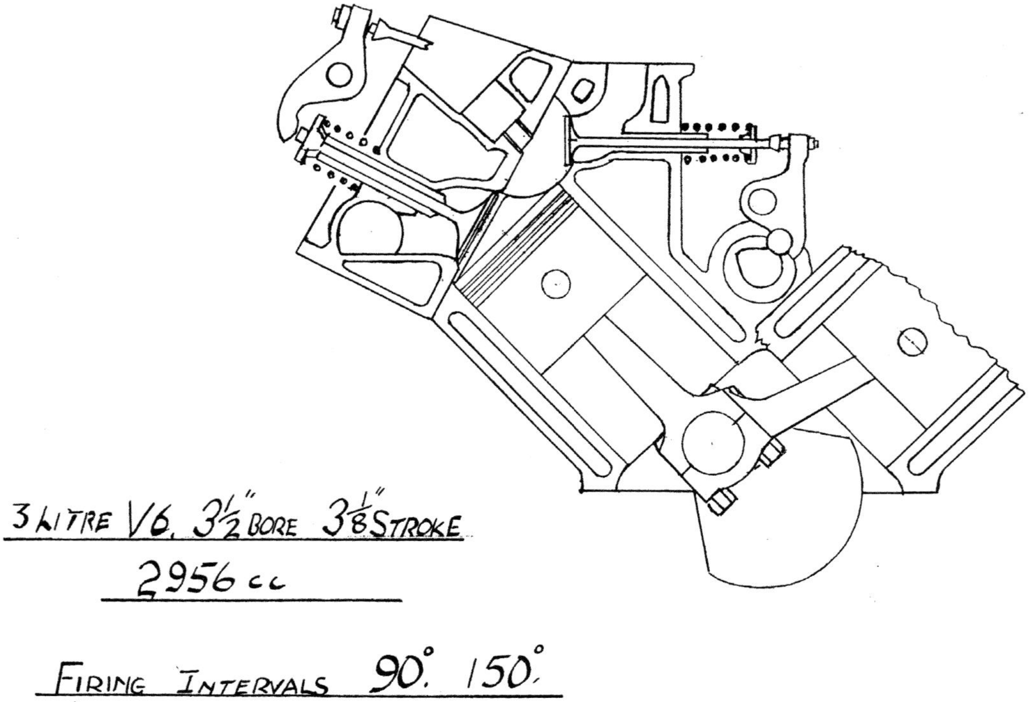

Jack Swaine's post-war V6 engine was drawn up in various sizes, including this 3-litre that was intended for the enlarged P5. Swaine drew this illustration many years later for an article in the Rover Sports Register's Freewheel *magazine.*

size as the contemporary Vauxhall Velox or Ford Zephyr Six, and it was to be aimed at roughly the same kind of customer.

Wilks also wanted to make use of an idea by the head of production engineering, Olaf Poppe, to dispense with traditional separate-chassis construction and use a rigid steel skeleton framework to which running gear and unstressed skin panels would be bolted. As for the engine, he was intrigued by the V6 engine of the Lancia Aurelia introduced in May 1950 (which was the world's first series production V6), and he asked Jack Swaine to resurrect the designs for a V6 engine he had been looking at in the late 1930s but to use the 60-degree cylinder bank angle that was key to the Lancia design. The engineering department tested several prototypes in P4s during 1952, and also obtained a Lancia Aurelia for examination.

By 1953, Wilks and his deputy, Robert Boyle, expected this new model to replace the P4 in the longer term, probably after an initial period in which the two were available alongside one another. As part of the preliminary work, Rover's new styling engineer, David Bache, was asked to draw up some styling proposals.

However, the new small Rover never reached production – or at least, not in the form originally intended. By summer 1954 the expansion of Land-Rover production had been such that Rover management realised they could not cope with a new high-volume car at that stage. So the P5 project was re-imagined as a low-volume luxury car positioned above the P4, and eventually entered production in 1958 as the Rover 3-litre. The ambitious thinking about construction that had come from Olaf Poppe eventually came to fruition as well, when that method of construction was used for the P6 range of 1963 that eventually replaced the P4.

APPENDIX I

Who was Who at Rover?

Very many individuals had an input into the management of Rover and into its products during the period that this book covers. However, the names of the leading lights occur several times, and as an easy source of reference this Appendix lists them in alphabetical order.

First, however, it is important to understand the structure and organisation of the Rover Company. It was guided from the top by a board of directors, whose numbers varied between five and six and who were responsible for setting policy and for guiding the company's business in order to meet agreed objectives.

The major areas or departments of the company included engineering, production, and sales. Each one of these major departments was broken down into sub-departments, although the precise breakdown (and the associated job titles) varied over the years. Thus, the engineering department included the drawing office, the experimental department, the development department, the engines department and the transmissions department. Slightly separate from the rest was the gas turbine department. At the head of each of these was a senior engineer, who would report through the assistant chief engineer to the chief engineer. A new and important element in this period was the export division, which was established during 1946, apparently within the sales department.

Car designs typically originated as an idea by the chief engineer, who in this period was Maurice Wilks. The detailed design would be done in the drawing office and would then be passed to the development engineers, who would oversee construction of prototypes and their testing. Each development project would be headed by a senior engineer (again, the titles changed over the years), and he would have a deputy and a number of junior engineers working for him.

A typical development team might consist of no more than three or four people; it would be led by a project engineer, whose deputy would have the title of assistant project engineer, and there would be one or more technical assistants, who were typically young engineers fresh from a Rover apprenticeship. Testing would be overseen by the development engineers but mileage work (which focused on durability) would be entrusted to a team of dedicated test drivers. When a design was considered satisfactory and had received the Board approval that granted the necessary funds for manufacture, it would be passed to the production department, who would turn it into a new product for sale.

One final, albeit small, department needs to be mentioned. This was the despatch department. Completed vehicles were tested and inspected by staff attached to the production department and were then signed off and handed over to the despatch department, which was responsible for their onward transmission to Rover distributors or individual customers. It is the records of the despatch department that survive today in the archives of the British Motor Museum at Gaydon, and which are a valuable source of information about the Rover Company's products.

Rover People

Gordon BASHFORD

Gordon Bashford joined Rover as an office boy in the drawing office at Queen Victoria Road in 1930. Keen to improve himself, he enrolled for numerous night-school classes in engineering and in 1934 briefly left Rover to gain wider experience at Alfred Herbert, the big Coventry machine tool company. On return to Rover, he became involved in the design of the company's late-1930s cars, and after the war he became the company's senior 'package' designer, responsible for the basic layouts of everything from the P3 saloon and Land-Rover in 1947–48 up to the SD1 saloon in 1976.

Frank BELL

Frank (F. R.) Bell was a New Zealander who had worked for Rolls-Royce on jet engine development and was recruited to Rover at the end of the war to take charge of the gas turbine car project. He oversaw all gas turbine work until 1953, when he left Rover to become chief designer for Blackburn & General Aircraft.

THE ROVER BOARD, 1945–53

Chairman	E. Ransom Harrison
Vice-chairman	H. Howe Graham
Managing director	S. B. Wilks
Works director	Sir Geoffrey Savage (died in 1953)
Secretary	Frank Ward (to 1945) Subsequently George Farmer (former assistant secretary and chief accountant)
Technical director	Maurice Wilks (from 1950)

Robert BOYLE

Robert Boyle had been a draughtsman under Georges Roesch at Talbot, and joined Rover in 1929, becoming an assistant to Maurice Wilks in 1930. He left the company in 1933 to become chief experimental engineer at Morris Motors in Oxford and in 1936 became the head of that company's engines branch. He rejoined Rover in 1938 as assistant chief engineer, again working under Maurice Wilks, moved up to become chief engineer in the 1950s and then became executive director (engineering) in 1957.

Ted COMMANDER

Ted Commander was a central figure on the purchasing and stores side of the Rover business. He had joined J. K. Starley & Co (a Rover predecessor) as a junior clerk in 1896, and became a buyer in 1911. He then worked his way up to become chief buyer, retiring from that post in the early 1950s. In 1960, he was then invited to join the Board, and served two more years for the company.

John CULLEN

John Cullen was appointed as development manager on the Land-Rover project, working to project leader Arthur Goddard. He was recruited to David Brown Industries in 1954, where he worked on the design and development of a light 4 × 4 that was cancelled before production began.

George FARMER

L. G. T. (Lovedin George Thomas) Farmer joined Rover as an accountant in 1940 and became assistant company secretary in the same year. Between 1941 and 1944 he was assistant secretary and company accountant. Between 1945 and 1952 he was secretary (and company accountant). In 1953 he was appointed to the Board as commercial director (and secretary). In later years, he worked his way up to joint managing director and then became chairman in October 1963 after Maurice Wilks died. Later deputy chairman of British Leyland and chairman of Rover-Triumph, he became chairman of Zenith after he retired from BL in May 1973.

Arthur GODDARD

Arthur Goddard joined Rover at the end of World War II to assist with their Meteor tank engine programme. His direct approach and ability to get things done impressed Maurice Wilks, who moved him onto other jobs where he gained a broad engineering experience. In 1947, still a young engineer in his early twenties, Goddard was put in charge of the Land-Rover project. In 1952 he was appointed assistant chief engineer, and he oversaw all further work on the Land-Rover until 1957, when he was appointed technical director of the Girling brake company and left Rover.

Chris GOODE

Chris Goode had been the deputy to 'Bro' Ward during development of the original P4, and took over as head of the team for the 1952 models. He was later involved with the P5 models and during the 1960s specialised in safety matters.

H. HOWE GRAHAM

When Lloyds Bank asked for an independent investigation into Rover's affairs at the end of 1931, the man appointed for the task was H. Howe Graham, a partner in a Birmingham firm of accountants called Messrs Gibson and Ashford. He was formally appointed to the Board in 1934 and subsequently became its vice-chairman. Howe Graham was widely respected within Rover and in 1954, when Ransom Harrison retired, he took over as chairman, serving in that capacity until 1957 when the post was given to S. B. Wilks.

Scott IVERSON

Scott Iverson was a promising young Norwegian engineer who contributed to early work on the M Model.

Len JACKMAN

Len Jackman was Rover's long-serving works manager, who retired on 30 April 1947 at the age of 69 after 40 years of service to Rover. His son Bernard later became production director and then managing director of Rover.

Ben LOKER

The engineering of a new body design was the responsibility of Ben Loker (Herbert Joseph Loker). When he retired in the mid-1950s, he had the title of chief body designer, and the last new Rover he worked on was the P4 saloon.

Charles NEWSOME

Charles (C. T.) Newsome joined Rover in 1911 after completing an apprenticeship at the Daimler company. He was closely involved with motorcycles at first, and joined the RASC mechanical transport section during World War I, earning himself an OBE (Military) in 1918.

For a brief period in 1929–30, he oversaw design and engineering at Rover, bridging the gap between Peter Poppe's departure and the promotion of Maurice Wilks to chief engineer. In 1932, he set up the new Inspection and Quality Control system that would be vital to the company's future. He eventually retired in 1959 as executive director of quality after 48 years' association with Rover.

Sam OSTLER

After a period with Austin at Longbridge, A. S. (Sam) Ostler joined Rover in the production development department. He worked on the original Land-Rover body and also prepared drawings for the detail construction of the P4 body. By February 1963 he was chief designer, Cars.

Noel PENNY

Noel Penny worked as a scientist at the Atomic Energy Authority before joining Rover in May 1952 as a technical assistant in the gas turbines department. He became chief engineer of that department in 1958, and many years later set up his own business, Noel Penny Turbines, in Coventry.

Olaf POPPE

Olaf Poppe joined Rover in 1928, at a time when his father Peter Poppe was the company's chief engineer. He specialised in production and planning, and was responsible for the design of the 'Christmas tree' jig on which early Land-Rover chassis were made. He rose to become an executive director by the late 1960s.

Ted RADFORD

Ted Radford joined Rover as a member of the works engineers staff in 1921. He became a section foreman in 1931 and took charge of the company's move to its Helen Street works in Coventry during 1932. Some thirteen years later, he took on a similar role when Rover moved to their new Solihull headquarters. In 1951, he became assistant works engineer, Building, and retired from that position in 1966.

E. RANSOM HARRISON

Edwin Ransom Harrison was a partner in Ransom Harrison & Lewis, Incorporated Accountants of Sheffield, and was appointed to the Rover Board in April 1931 to fill the vacant directorship left by the death of Sir Alfred Mays-Smith. He was elected chairman in November 1932 and oversaw a particularly stable time at Rover until he retired in 1954.

W. J. ROBINSON

W. J. Robinson was an important figure on the production side at Rover. Usually known as 'Robo', he had started as a body maker at Rover's Parkside factory in August 1919 and then became foreman of the jig shop at Helen Street in the 1930s. By June 1939 he was assistant to works manager Len Jackman, and succeeded him as production manager when Jackman retired in 1948. From 1960, he became Rover's executive director (Production), and still held that post when he died in January 1969.

Sir Geoffrey SAVAGE

Geoffrey H. Savage was one of the many Rover people who joined the company from Hillman after that company was bought by the Rootes Brothers. He came to take charge of production in 1930, and became highly respected in his job. He was co-opted to the Rover Board in 1937 as works director, and was knighted in 1952 but sadly died the following year.

Roland SEALE

Roland (F. R. S.) Seale joined the company in 1922 with Peter Poppe as the latter's design assistant, and made important contributions to the design of Rovers from the 1920s into the 1960s. For much of that period, he was head of the drawing office. In his spare time, he wrote two books. One concerned his hobby of wood-turning, and the other combined poetry with physics and was called *The Rhyming Physicist*. Seale became known as 'George' from his habit of calling everybody George, which was the name he gave to his son. Some Rover people believed that this was the origin of the name George that was given to the Viking's head mascot on the P4 saloons of the 1950s. Seale retired with the title of chief designer in 1966 after 44 years with Rover.

Frank SHAW

Frank Shaw joined Rover from Rolls-Royce in 1943 to work on transmission design. At Rolls-Royce he had been on the team that turned the Merlin engine into the Meteor. He later became the chief engineer in charge of the transmission department.

Brian SILVESTER

Brian Silvester joined Rover in 1949 and became a research engineer, later heading the company's research department.

A. B. SMITH

A. B. Smith joined Rover in the stores department in 1925 and then became a buyer at the Tyseley factory in 1934. Known to friends as Bernard but to his Rover colleagues as 'A. B.', he became buyer and stores controller for the Rover shadow factories between 1936 and 1946. He took over from Ted Commander as Rover's chief buyer in the 1950s, became general manager in 1962 and then managing director in 1969. The next step up was to chairman in 1973, and he retired in 1975 when Rover ceased to exist as a separate company. In later years, he was immensely respected by Rover employees as a gentleman and the last of the 'old' Rover people.

Jack SWAINE

John ('Jack') Swaine effectively stepped into Robert Boyle's shoes when the latter left Rover in 1933, taking on primary responsibility for engine design. Towards the end of the 1930s, he drew up the new IOE engine that would become Rover's staple after the war, and he remained in charge of Rover engine design right through until his retirement in the 1970s.

C. A. 'Bro' WARD

C. A. 'Bro' Ward was the engineer who led the P4 development team.

Frank WARD

Frank Ward was a major figure on the Rover Board right through the period covered by this book. He had joined J. K. Starley & Co in 1889 and was appointed company secretary in 1902. He was caretaking the role of general manager before the arrival of S. B. Wilks in 1929, when his role was redefined as company secretary and chief accountant. He joined the Board as a director in 1932 and retired in 1953 after completing an astonishing 64 years' unbroken service with Rover.

Maurice WILKS

Maurice Fernand Cary Wilks had learned the motor business through two years at General Motors in the USA before joining Hillman as a planning engineer. He followed his older brother Spencer Wilks to Rover, where he was appointed as chief engineer to succeed Peter Poppe in 1930. His first job was to run the Scarab project, but within a couple of years he was having a major impact on engineering policy at Rover, and was the driving force behind all Rover engineering in the 1930s.

Maurice Wilks was responsible for the concept of the Land-Rover in 1947, and was appointed to the Rover Board as a director in 1950. He was always an innovative engineer, leading Rover into experiments with gas turbine propulsion in the late 1940s and fostering a company culture in which new ideas were able to thrive. After he became joint managing director in 1956 and chairman in 1962, he continued to influence Rover and Land-Rover engineering. Maurice Wilks died in 1963 as a widely respected figure within the motor industry.

S. B. WILKS

Spencer Bernau Wilks, usually known as S. B., had been joint managing director at the Hillman company but had left after the Rootes takeover in 1928. Wilks was a lawyer by training, had risen to the rank of captain in the army during the war and had married one of William Hillman's daughters. He was appointed as general manager at Rover in September 1929 and subsequently joined the Board as a director. He became managing director in 1933 and his steady hand is rightly credited with much of the success of Rover in the later 1930s and beyond. In 1956, he shared the position of managing director with his brother, Maurice Wilks, and in 1957 became Rover's chairman. He handed over to his brother in 1962 but remained on the Rover Board, and became the company's life president in 1967. S. B. Wilks died in 1971.

Jess WORSTER

Jess Worster was another of the many engineers who joined Rover from Hillman, and his first job for his new employers in 1930 was as a planning engineer. He became works manager at Tyseley in 1932 and followed a career on the production side of the company. He became executive director (Production) in 1957 and a full director the following year. Although he retired in February 1965, he remained on the Board until July and spent his final three months on secondment to Rover South Africa where he oversaw that company's expansion. He was well liked and was known to employees for his characteristic fedora hat; his son, Nigel Worster, followed in his footsteps as a Rover apprentice.

APPENDIX II

The Rover Factories

All the Rovers and Land-Rovers covered in this book were manufactured at the company's factory in Lode Lane, Solihull, about 10 miles south-east of Birmingham, which had been built in 1939–40 as a wartime 'shadow' factory.

Solihull

Germany's increasingly aggressive stance after Hitler came to power in 1933 made clear that it was only a matter of time before there would be another war in Europe, and from 1936 the British government began to prepare for what it saw as an inevitability. As re-armament began in earnest that year, it also became clear that the existing aero engine manufacturers would not be able to increase production quickly enough to provide all the aircraft that the Royal Air Force would need. So the Air Ministry devised a plan that became known as the Shadow Factory scheme. It called for a series of new factories to be built to 'shadow' or duplicate the existing aero engine plants. These new factories were to be financed by the government but would be managed on their behalf by major industrial concerns.

In April 1936, the Rover Company was one of seven Coventry car makers who were asked to join the shadow factory scheme. Its first shadow factory was built at Acocks Green (*see* below) and was operational by summer 1937. Solihull was the second – and for a long time was known to Rover as Shadow Factory no 2. At this stage, Rover's headquarters were at Helen Street in Coventry, which was also where the cars were built; part of that factory was also given over to work on aero engines after war was declared in 1939.

The contract with the government allowed the companies that managed these shadow factories to have first refusal on them when they were no longer needed. As the Helen Street factory had been damaged in the Blitz during 1940 and would need to be modernised anyway, Rover chose to move to Solihull. The factory was not initially made available to purchase, but the Ministry of Aircraft Production agreed a ten-year lease that expired in September 1955.

The factory was very much larger than Rover's old Helen Street premises, and in the beginning there were some doubts whether the company would ever be able to fill it. However, once the Land-Rover came on-stream, there were no longer any doubts, and the question from then on was how the company could fund more assembly areas to meet demand.

Solihull remained the headquarters and primary factory of the Rover Company until 1978, when it was taken over by the newly-formed Land Rover Ltd. It has remained central to that company's operations ever since, is now owned by JLR (Jaguar Land Rover), and also assembles some Jaguar models.

Acocks Green

Rover's Acocks Green factory was on Clay Lane, on the road between Solihull and Birmingham, and about 4 miles south-east of Birmingham city centre. It was always known as Acocks Green to avoid confusion with the other Clay Lane premises, which were in Coventry.

In its early days, Acocks Green was known to Rover as its No 1 Shadow Factory, as it was the first of the shadow factories that the company was asked to manage on behalf of the Air Ministry. Its original purpose was to produce parts for the Bristol aircraft engines used in military aircraft. The factory was built on the site of a former market gardening business (called Westwood's), near the canal. Construction began in 1936, and the factory was operational by July 1937.

In February 1939, the Midlands Co-Operative Society opened a laundry nearby, and this was taken over by Rover in April 1942 to increase production space. In conjunction with Lucas, Rover at Acocks Green built half-a-dozen jet engines, but after the factory had been hit three times by Luftwaffe bombing (on the nights of 19–20, 22–23 November and 11–12 December 1940), the decision was made to move this programme to some disused cotton mills in Lancashire. The move took place in spring 1941.

When the war ended, Rover was able to retain the Acocks Green factory, which it used primarily for building the Meteor and Meteorite tank and military-vehicle engines under government contract (*see* Appendix V). The former Co-Op building was meanwhile returned to its owners and became a laundry again. The government contracts ended in 1964, and Acocks Green then became Rover's primary engine plant. It also became the home of the technical films department (the Rover photographic section), and later passed into the ownership of Land Rover Ltd.

Clay Lane

Rover had a complicated association with a group of small factory buildings at Clay Lane in the Stoke Row area of Coventry. The company bought one that had been used by Midland Light Bodies (who built some bodies as an independent coachbuilder on Rover chassis). One of the adjacent buildings had been the workshops of coachbuilder Cross & Ellis up to 1938, when it was bought from the receiver by AP Aircraft Ltd. After the war, AP Aircraft would build the bodies for the 1947 Rover Tourers, and for that purpose rented part of the Rover-owned building next door.

When Rover moved to Solihull in 1945 and abandoned its Coventry premises, Ransom Harrison arranged for a small service department to be set up in the company's buildings at Clay Lane in order to provide maintenance facilities for those Rover customers who had been accustomed to getting their cars maintained at the old service department in Coventry. In the mid-1960s, this service department moved from Clay Lane to the Alvis service department at Jobs Lane, Coventry, and then closed on 28 June 1968; its functions were taken over by recently appointed Rover distributors S. H. Newsome & Co Ltd.

Perry Barr

During expansion made necessary by the success of the Land-Rover, Rover bought an existing factory in the north-west Birmingham suburb of Perry Barr. The factory was on the corner of Wellhead Lane and Birchfield Road, and became the centre for manufacture of Land-Rover axles. It was closed in 1983 and the site was sold for redevelopment.

Seagrave Road

Seagrave Road was not a factory but was the Rover service depot in Fulham, south-west London. Its purpose was to maintain cars on behalf of London customers, but it was also used as a staging-post for vehicles shipped abroad on company business (including the Land-Rovers displayed at Amsterdam in 1948), and became the home of the Royal Review Land-Rovers. The site has since been redeveloped.

Springfield

Rover bought the 17,000sq ft factory of the former Springfield Joinery Works in early 1952 as part of its expansion plan. This was close to the Serck Radiators plant on the Warwick Road in Birmingham. It became the Rover tool room and was used for the manufacture of prototype parts until it was closed down in the early 1980s.

Tyseley (Tyseley 1)

The Tyseley factory was at King's Road and Hay Hall Road, near the Tyseley locomotive works in Birmingham. This had been a government munitions factory during World War I, and Rover had bought it (probably in 1919) for building the air-cooled Eight. It was expanded in 1930.

Collins & Stratton explain in *British Car Factories from 1896* that a central roadway divided the Tyseley site into two sections. The main machine and assembly shops were on one side, while the heat treatment and enamelling shops were on the other side, together with the woodworking department. The main stores were adjacent to the roadway. The chassis line ran along one of the outside boundaries of the main building. During 1931 (when Rover were increasing production dramatically), the works was producing 400 cars a week and employed 1,100 people.

The Tyseley factory remained in Rover ownership as a components factory, but in more recent years belonged to Land Rover Ltd. It was demolished after closure and is now the site of the Rovex Business Park. The Rover mosaic logo in the floor of the old entrance has been preserved in its original position. Note that Land-Rover actually operated two factories in Tyseley; the other, which was known as Tyseley 2, was adjacent to the original premises and was bought from the Co-Operative Wholsesale Society in 1969.

APPENDIX III

Rover CKD Operations, 1948–53

By 1948 the British motor industry had been told that companies which failed to sell 75 per cent of their products overseas would risk losing their rationed supplies of steel. This ruling must have put severe pressure on Rover. They did not yet know whether their new Land-Rover was going to attract the export sales they needed, but they did know that their new P3 saloon models were unlikely to do so, because they were too old-fashioned in style to compete with more modern designs from manufacturers outside the UK.

It was now vitally important to investigate all means of increasing export sales, and among the options that Rover investigated was overseas assembly from CKD. (The initials stand for 'Completely Knocked Down', and the system involves kits of parts manufactured in the country of origin being shipped to an overseas plant for assembly into a complete car; sometimes, locally produced items such as paint, tyres or batteries may be incorporated.)

The late 1940s brought new conditions that favoured the proliferation of such overseas assembly operations. Several undeveloped countries around the world had been touched by the 1939–45 war and had recognised the value of mechanical transport for the first time. They recognised the advantage of having their own motor industries, and some welcomed full manufacturing operations set up by established overseas companies. Others lacked the skills base and saw assembly as a way of building up the necessary skills before progressing to full local manufacture.

Rover had to learn the ropes very quickly. The company had last had an overseas assembly operation in 1930–31, and the experience had not been a happy one. The operation in New Zealand had foundered when changes in exchange rates destroyed its viability. Such risks would always be present, but the normally risk-averse Rover management decided that they were less of a threat to the company's survival than the more immediate threat of being denied supplies of steel. It is perhaps odd that discussions did not take place in the boardroom, but at a lower level of management. One way or another, there is no direct reference to the new overseas assembly venture in the Rover Board minutes of the period.

The preparations for the company's new CKD operation must have been made in early 1948. The new P3 saloons had not been designed with CKD in mind, and nor had the new Land-Rover. Nevertheless, the export department and the manufacturing department had to get together to work out a way of shipping the Rover products in kit form, while negotiations went ahead to establish the assembly plants themselves. The evidence suggests that the company was still learning as its CKD operation got under way shortly before Easter 1948.

The first CKD arrangements were made with India and Eire. In India, the long process of independence from British colonial rule had come to an end in August 1947, and the country was as yet far from stable. Against this background, Rover came to an agreement with its Indian agents, Dewars Garage & Engineering Works in Calcutta, to assemble cars from CKD kits. In Eire, the Rover agency was held by Lincoln & Nolan of Dublin, and this company had already established a small assembly operation for the products of other British car makers. It was therefore relatively simple for Rover to join in.

The CKD P3 Saloons

The CKD arrangements for the P3 saloons were ready several months before those for Land-Rovers. Only the six-light saloons were made available in CKD form, perhaps because of anticipated demand or perhaps purely to simplify the logistics at Rover's end. The very first ones were 75 models that left Solihull for Calcutta on 18 March 1948, and these appear to have been joined in April by two fully-built 75 Saloons to act as samples. They were followed by the first 60 models on 21 April, and more batches of both types followed over the next eighteen months or so. In total, Dewars received 210 75 Saloons and 66 60 Saloons in kit form. Sadly, no evidence of the success or otherwise of the completed cars among buyers in India has yet come to light.

From the beginning, the CKD sets were shipped in batches of six, apparently because this made the most economical use of shipping space. The records of the despatch department show that the bodies were already painted before leaving Solihull, so presumably Dewars did not at that stage have a paint shop that could handle the process. No pictures have been discovered so far, but no doubt the bodies were carefully packed into wooden crates with other, smaller items around them. Chassis frames were perhaps stacked in other crates; engines, gearboxes and so on in yet others. On arrival in Calcutta, the crates would have been broken open and their contents arranged in some kind of store before being moved to what was almost certainly a slow-moving assembly line with almost no automation at all.

CKD deliveries to Dublin began in late May 1948 with 75 Saloons, and were supplemented by the first 60s in October. Like the cars for India, these were shipped in batches of six and their bodies had been painted at Solihull. However, beginning in December 1948 the bodies were delivered in Primer, which must indicate that the Lincoln & Nolan operation had now moved on to painting the bodies itself. Whether it used standard Rover colours or not is unfortunately not recorded. As with the Indian operation, two fully-built sample cars were sent to Dublin alongside the CKD deliveries. Lincoln & Nolan received 36 examples of the 75 Saloon in CKD form and 30 examples of the 60 before deliveries ended in summer 1949.

From April 1949, a third country became involved in CKD assembly of P3 Saloons. This was New Zealand, which took only examples of the 75 model. The arrangements here were different again, and the CKD sets were delivered to each of Rover's four regional distributors in the country. Two of these were on the South Island (Broadway Parking & Petrol Station at Dunedin and Christchurch Car Exchange at Christchurch) and two on the North Island (Khyber Pass Motors of Auckland and Wellington Motors of Wellington). All four had received at least one fully-built 75 Saloon each during 1948, and Broadway and Christchurch received a total of six cars each while the other two each had a dozen, making the total of CKD exports to New Zealand up to 36. Once again, no contemporary reports on the assembly operations or on the assembled cars have yet been found.

All the CKD P3 models were numbered within the standard chassis sequences, and all their chassis numbers would at least theoretically have had an R prefix to indicate a right-hand-drive export model.

The CKD Land-Rovers

The CKD Land-Rover operations did not start until the autumn of 1949, after those for the P3 Saloons had ended. By this stage, Rover must have had a good idea of how to make the system work most efficiently, and of course the simpler construction of the Land-Rover must have made preparation of the CKD sets considerably easier than it had been for the cars. The 1950-season CKD Land-Rovers had chassis numbers within the standard sequences, just as the P3 Saloons had done, but for the 1951 and later seasons they were given their own separate sequences, with separate ones for RHD and LHD types.

The first two countries to assemble Land-Rovers from CKD were Australia and India. The Indian operation again depended on Dewars Garage in Calcutta, who by this time had around eighteen months' experience of assembling the P3 Saloons. Shipping from Solihull began in September 1949 with 0610-series models and continued later in the season with 0611-series types. No 1951 models were sent to India, for reasons that are not clear, but shipments resumed in around August 1951 and Dewars went on to assemble examples of the 1952 and 1953 2-litre 80s.

The Australian operation was more complex, and probably drew on experience gained relatively recently with P3 assembly in New Zealand. The vast size of the country had led Rover to establish five master distributors in different regions, each with exclusive rights over geographical areas that did not quite follow state borders. Regent Motors of Melbourne covered Victoria and Tasmania; Champions Ltd of Adelaide covered South Australia and the Northern Territory; Faulls Motors of Perth covered Western Australia; Grenville Motors of Sydney covered most of New South Wales and the Australian Capital Territory; and Annand & Thompson covered Queensland and the Northern Rivers region of New South Wales.

Four of these master distributors took CKD kits and assembled them in-house, but Faulls did not have the necessary facilities and so took fully-built export Land-Rovers. At least two of the master distributors added their own distinctive touches: Annand & Thompson stencilled the Land-Rover name in yellow onto the front and rear of the Land-Rovers they distributed, and Grenville Motors attached their own metal badge to the left front wing of each Land-Rover.

Late in the 1950 season Lincoln & Nolan in Eire received their first Land-Rover sets for assembly. As happened with the Indian operation, there were no CKD shipments during the 1951 season, but the company resumed Land-Rover assembly for the 1952 and 1953 seasons and would continue to build Land-Rovers beyond that. Quantities were nevertheless always small, and sometimes tiny.

More Land-Rover assembly operations began to spring up at the start of the 1950s. Records suggest that CKD Land-Rovers were sent to Denmark during the 1950 and 1951 seasons, but it has been impossible to find out any more about this, and some authorities doubt whether a Danish assembly operation ever existed. One way or another, Denmark definitely received Land-Rovers numbered in LHD CKD sequences during those years. Further new operations appear to have been set up in South Africa in 1950 and in Mexico in 1952.

Research continues into these overseas assembly operations, and at present the only evidence for their existence is that despatch records show South Africa and Mexico as destinations for Land-Rovers numbered as CKD types. The South African operation was probably at Port Elizabeth and the records suggest it received 1666-series models in the 1951 model-year and 3666-series models in the 1953 model-year; there is no indication that any 1952 models were sent there. The Mexican assembly plant received more than 430 Land-Rovers in the 1952 and 1953 seasons, but its exact location has not been identified.

Perhaps emboldened by the success of its CKD business, Rover established the first of another type of overseas assembly operation during 1952 when it began supplying part-completed Land-Rovers to Minerva in Belgium; a similar arrangement with Tempo in West Germany was set up in 1953.

The CKD P4 Saloons

CKD assembly of the P4 saloons followed logically from that of the P3 saloons, but only after a long delay. This was probably caused by difficulties in getting the new models into production: although announced in September 1949, they were not available in quantity until around Easter 1950.

The P4 models were assembled in three overseas locations during this period. Lincoln & Nolan assembled them in Eire during the 1951, 1952 and 1953 seasons; Dewar's Garage in Calcutta, India, began with late 1950 models and continued into 1953 and beyond; and the only LHD examples were assembled in Belgium by Anciens Etablissements Pilette, the Rover agents in Brussels, for the 1952 and 1953 seasons. Unfortunately, the despatch records for the 1952 season seem to be incomplete, and there may have been another eighteen cars, whose destinations are not known.

The earliest CKD P4s were 1950-model Cyclops types, of which five went to Dewars in Calcutta during October 1950. The same company took a further 84 of the 1951 models for local assembly. There were more 1951 Cyclops for Eire, and a total of 42 CKD sets were shipped there.

The quantities of CKD P4s remained small during the 1952 and 1953 season. Right-hand-drive 75s went to India (36 in 1952 and six in 1953) and to Eire (eighteen in 1952 and 58 in 1953), and in late 1953 a few 60s and 90s went to Eire, where at least some of them were completed with a two-tone colour split that was unavailable anywhere else in the world. The known left-hand-drive models were all 75s for Belgium (72 in the 1952 season and 90 more in 1953). Belgium had taken fully-built LHD cars during the 1951 season, and reverted to fully-built P4s again for 1954, and the reasons for its brief CKD interlude are not known.

APPENDIX IV

The Marauder

The Marauder was a short-lived sports car that was based on the chassis and running-gear of the Rover P4 75. Just fifteen examples were built between 1950 and 1952, and most of them still survive today.

By the standards of the late 1940s, the P4 75 had good handling and performance, and this prompted three young Rover engineers to draw up plans for a three-seater sports derivative on a modified version of its chassis. All three – George Mackie, Peter Wilks and Spen King – were motor racing enthusiasts, and had in fact already built a successful single-seater racer from a redundant Rover development chassis in 1948 (*see* Chapter 1).

Their original and rather vague plan was to build an open two-seater with cycle wings, but the plan changed after George Mackie, then based in Brussels as Rover's continental representative, was impressed by the full-width styling of a Ferrari 166 that he saw at the Geneva Show in March 1949. That car must have been the one-off 166 Inter with Farina drophead bodywork, which had chassis number 011S.

The new P4 75 was launched in September 1949, and Mackie lost no time in modifying a picture of it to look like a sleek two-door sports tourer. He glued the result on a postcard and sent it to Peter Wilks, and it was this picture that heavily influenced the eventual appearance of the car, which Wilks and King now set about designing with the assistance of Richard Mead, owner of a small coachbuilding concern in Dorridge, near Solihull.

Peter Wilks and George Mackie decided to leave Rover and to set up in business to build the car in quantity. King, who was then working on the final stages of the gas turbine car that would become JET 1, decided to stay where he was, but put money into the project and continued to lend active support. The trio secured Rover agreement for a supply of the Rover chassis and engines that formed the basis of their design, and used their contacts to persuade eight Rover distributors to sell and service the cars. They decided to call the car a Marauder.

With capital provided by all three principals and by Peter Wilks' father, Geoffrey (GL) Wilks, who became a fourth director, Wilks, Mackie and Company opened for business on 1 January 1950. They rented offices at Richard Mead's premises in Poplar Road, Dorridge and continued to work on the design of the Marauder until the first P4 chassis arrived from the Rover Company on 9 March. Friends and acquaintances lent a hand from time to time: gas turbine man Noel Penny

Some 40 years after it was built, George Mackie bought back Marauder number 11007 and treated it to a thorough restoration. It is now displayed in the British Motor Museum at Gaydon.

remembered (in John Mortimer's book, *Automotive Gas Turbines*) that the electrics were developed by Geoffrey Middleton, who later worked with him in the gas turbine division.

A determined effort had the first Marauder completed in July 1950, by which time a second chassis had also been delivered and work had begun on that. After early tests around local roads, Wilks and Mackie took the prototype on a long-distance test through Belgium, Luxembourg and Switzerland, where nothing worse than gearbox lubrication problems showed up. In the course of the ten-day trip, the pair called on the Swiss Rover importers, who invited them to show a Marauder on the Rover stand at the 1951 Geneva motor show. They accepted with enthusiasm!

Back in Britain, the prototype was introduced to the motoring press in August at the Dorridge Hotel, and the first orders began to come in from those Rover distributors who had accepted Marauder franchises. Wilks, Mackie and Company generated cash-flow by a stage-payments scheme: they allocated a chassis number to each firm order and then invoiced the distributor for his chassis when it was complete. The balance then became payable when the body had been built and the car was ready.

The Rover 75 chassis was shortened to give a 102in wheelbase for the Marauder; a 9-inch section was cut out just ahead of the upsweep over the rear wheels. Repositioned cross-members allowed the engine to be mounted 19in further back and 2 inches lower in the frame, where it was set horizontally rather than sloping backwards as in the parent saloon. This improved the weight distribution to give better handling, and also took weight off the front wheels so that higher-geared and more sporty steering could be fitted. The steering box was moved back and the drop arm lengthened to suit, giving a quick two turns lock-to-lock instead of the P4's four turns.

George Mackie and Peter Wilks were photographed in Berne with the prototype Marauder during their continental test run in 1950.

There were also some suspension modifications, partly to improve the car's handling and partly because of the repositioned cross-members.

Meanwhile, the twin-carburettor engine was mildly uprated from its standard 75bhp form to deliver 80bhp at the same 4,200rpm. A thinner head gasket raised the compression ratio to around 7.6:1, and the valve springs were packed with washers to eliminate valve bounce. The Rover gearbox was retained, but its column-change gave way to a short floor-mounted gear-stick, positioned 6 inches off the car's centre-line towards the driver. The prototype Marauder also dispensed with the Rover freewheel, and instead had an overdrive unit manufactured by H. and A. Engineering of Croydon; this was removed from the car after its trip to Europe in 1950, and few production Marauders were delivered with overdrive, which was offered as an extra-cost option. The axle was the standard P4 item, with its 4.3:1 overall gearing.

The two-seat tourer body was built from steel around a shortened 75 floor pan, with bonnet, boot lid, doors, scuttle and cowl made from weight-saving aluminium. Despite the two-door configuration, it was unmistakably related to the parent Rover saloon. The out-turned lower edges of the body had stainless steel capping strips exactly like the P4's, and the shape of the wheel arches again recalled the parent saloon. Yet the front wings and two-piece bonnet had been redesigned around the lower-mounted engine to give a less upright profile, and although the rear again recalled the P4, it actually incorporated a rather impractical locker instead of a proper boot. At the front, a wide radiator grille helped to make the

This Marauder was photographed while under construction at the Dorridge works of Wilks, Mackie & Co, probably in 1951.

car look low and sleek, and carried a grille badge with a flaming torch motif, which was designed by George Mackie's wife Rosemary.

Finding a buyer for the prototype Marauder generated much-needed funds for the new company. It was sold to Bernard Willmott, the owner of Willmotts Rover dealership in Bognor Regis. He and his wife had been using Rovers in competition since the 1930s, and on his first outing with the Marauder Willmott took a class second in the November 1950 *Daily Express* 1000 Miles Rally. The Willmotts also entered the first production car, chassis number 11001, in the Isle of Wight Rally and hill climb during April 1951, this time coming third in their class. Shortly afterwards, in June 1951, Peter Wilks himself claimed second place – to no less a driver than the young Mike Hawthorn – in a five-lap handicap at Goodwood.

These competition appearances and a favourable write-up in *The Autocar* of 22 June 1951 provided valuable publicity, but there were two factors that hindered sales. The first was that the car was too expensive, costing around 12 to 15 per cent more than a standard Rover 75 saloon. It also cost rather more than a Jaguar XK120, the sports car sensation of the time. The second factor was that the Marauder lacked performance. In the hands of *The Autocar*, the overdrive-equipped demonstrator (chassis number 11006) could not better 89mph and 0–60mph in 18.4 seconds. The XK120, by comparison, had a top speed of 120mph and could reach 60mph from rest in 9 seconds!

The next logical development of the Marauder was to improve that performance, and Wilks, Mackie & Co did so in two ways. On the one hand, they bored out the engine to take the readily

The Marauder grille badge was designed by George Mackie's wife.

available 69.5mm pistons from the 1595cc engine of the P3 60. This achieved 100bhp from 2393cc and was logically called the Marauder 100 specification. On the other hand, they developed a triple-carburettor head, with a cast manifold like that tried experimentally on a handful of P3 75 saloons during the development of the P4 early in 1949. It is not clear how much power was achieved with this, but the two options could be combined, and the company demonstrator (Marauder 11006) was so converted.

All these promising upgrades were announced in March 1951, when 11006 was shown at Geneva, but they had precious little time to make any impact. The April 1951 Budget imposed a new double purchase tax of $66\frac{2}{3}$ per cent on cars with a basic cost of over £1,000. Other costs were already rising, and the Marauder's makers were unable to keep below that £1,000 ceiling for even the standard car. As a result, the price of a new Marauder in standard trim shot up to £2,002 inclusive of purchase tax, which was almost £400 more expensive than a Jaguar XK120 two-seater.

Faced with that unpleasant reality, Wilks, Mackie and Company nevertheless chose to press on doggedly. In July 1951, they signed a contract for their own premises in Kenilworth, and when they moved in early in 1952 changed their name to the Marauder Car Company Ltd. By this time, eight or nine Marauders had gone to customers, and body production had been transferred from Richard Mead's premises to Abbey Panels in Coventry. Mead nevertheless continued to paint and trim the Marauder bodies, and those built

Approval from above: demonstrator 11006 was photographed outside the house where Rover's managing director S. B. Wilks lived.

by Abbey Panels were indistinguishable from his originals. Unfortunately, they were also some two hundredweight (102kg) heavier, which was no help to a car that was already underpowered in standard form.

Even so, the Abbey Panels bodies built after October 1951 did incorporate some worthwhile improvements. They featured a separate adjustable driver's seat in place of the original bench seat, thus giving the driver greater comfort and allowing the back of the passenger seat to be folded flat to improve access to the luggage locker from inside the car.

In the optimistic belief that the Marauder might find buyers overseas, the twelfth car (chassis number 11011) was built towards the end of 1951 with left-hand drive. It was shipped out to the Paris showrooms of the French Rover importer, Franco-Britannic Autos, but did not find a buyer and was brought back to the UK and converted to right-hand drive. Somewhat ironically, it was then bought by an American, who nevertheless agreed to take the car with its steering wheel on the right.

Meanwhile, some help was at hand. The Rover Board stepped in, and at its January 1952 meeting discussed taking a financial interest in the company, in view of the possibility of US sales. They agreed that the best solution was to acquire the new factory, and in February bought it for £3,900 and agreed to lease it to the Marauder Car Company.

It was a hugely supportive gesture, but it came too late. The Marauder Car Company called it a

The last Marauder to be completed was this unique fixed-head coupé.

day in the middle of 1952, after fifteen Marauder-badged cars had been built. The last car, numerically, was delivered to Henlys of London on 26 March 1952, and the last car to be completed – a unique fixed-head coupé version bearing chassis number 12004 and ordered in the closing months of 1950 – reached its new owner a month after that. By September 1952, the assets of the company had been sold.

Marauders continued to appear in competition, most notably in the hands of Frank Shanks, who campaigned the triple-carburettor demonstrator, 11006, vigorously during 1952–53. However, Marauders were simply not competitive in club events, and the marque gradually disappeared from view over the next few years.

As for the Marauder's creators, George Mackie returned to Rover, where he later became head of the Land-Rover special projects department, and Peter Wilks spent some time with Rover dealers Gethin's in Tyseley before rejoining Rover. He took over as the company's chief engineer in 1964. Spen King remained with the Rover gas turbines division until the early 1960s, and eventually became technical director for British Leyland.

THE MARAUDER, 1950–51

Some details of the fifteen Marauders have still not been discovered, 70 years after they were built. This table lists what was known at the time of writing. Some of the surviving cars have been modified over the years.

Car no	*Reg no*	*Year built*	
PRO1/1	KAC 313	1950	Prototype Marauder. Survives.
11001	MBP 2	1950	Survives.
11002			No details known, but *see* note below.
11003	BSN 823	1951	Survives.
12004	MOE 645	1952	Fixed-head coupé. Survives.
11005	OUG 777	1951	Survives.
11006	KWD 111	1951	Tested by *The Autocar* and shown at Geneva in 1951 before conversion to Marauder 100 specification with triple-carburettor option. Survives.
11007	HFY 330	1951	Survives, after restoration by George Mackie in the 1980s.
11008	LTL 1, then VCT 257		May have had another registration before LTL 1. Fitted with removable hardtop. Survives.
11009	RKC 762	1951	Survives.
11010	NBP 313	1951	Survives.
11011	IOWA 20202	1951	Marauder 100 specification. Survives, in the USA.
11012	FHE 437	1952	Believed scrapped in 1967.
11013	MOL 629	1952	Survives.
11014		1952	No details known.

The fifteen Rover 75 chassis delivered to Wilks, Mackie & Company (or the Marauder Car Co) in 1950–51 were as follows:

0430-0519	1430-0599	1430-1145
0430-2041	1430-0600	1430-1824
0430-2042	1430-1009	1430-1825
0430-4692	1430-1010	1430-1949
0430-4716	1430-1144	1430-1950

The Marauders retained their original Rover engine numbers.

Marauder 11002: There is no hard information about this car, although a one-off special registered in December 1950 and built by a Marauder Car Company would theoretically fit the bill. An advertisement for it in *Motor Sport* of the mid-1950s describes it as having a body resembling a Jaguar XK120, wire wheels, a tuned 4-litre Ford Mercury V8 and a Columbia dual-range back axle. It was built for Lord Keyes at a cost of £3,000. George Mackie did not recall any such car when asked in the mid-1990s, and Lord Keyes could remember very little about it.

APPENDIX V

Meteors and Meteorites

Throughout the period covered by this book, and right up until 1964, Rover built Meteor tank engines on behalf of the British government at its Acocks Green factory. The programme was initially undertaken on behalf of the Ministry of Supply (MoS), and the Acocks Green plant was for many years known locally as 'Rover MoS'. In all, Rover built about 9,000 Meteor engines, and also developed and produced the Meteorite derivative for heavy haulage vehicles.

Rover's involvement with tank engines began during World War II. The company had initially been asked to work with Frank Whittle on development of his jet aero engine, but relations between Rover and Whittle's Power Jets Ltd became strained. Meanwhile, Rolls-Royce had showed an interest in becoming involved with the jet engine work. In late 1942, the Air Ministry therefore brokered a deal, under which Rover would hand over all work on the Whittle jet to Rolls-Royce, and in return would be given full ownership of the Rolls-Royce Meteor tank engine programme. Meteor production was moved into Rover's Acocks Green No1 Shadow Factory, and would remain there until the end.

The Meteor was of course the 27-litre V12 engine developed from the hugely successful Rolls-Royce Merlin aero engine that first ran in the 1930s and went on to become a staple of the Royal Air Force. The idea of turning it into a tank engine came from Leyland Motors in 1940, when that company was co-operating with Rolls-Royce on tank design. The aero engine's supercharger was removed, its direction of rotation was changed to suit automotive practice, and some components were redeveloped to use steel instead of the precious aluminium originally used to save weight. The first Meteor was tested in a tank at Aldershot in April 1941 and delivered about 600bhp when running on pool petrol. It was exactly what the army needed.

Rover took on the project in two stages, initially joining Morris in 1943 to build Meteor engines when demand proved too much for Meadows engines, who had been the primary manufacturer. Then from January 1944, Rover took over primary responsibility for the engine, and later types were correctly known as Rover Meteor engines, although they were often still referred to as Rolls-Royce types.

The demand for Meteor tank engines continued long past the end of the war, not least because they were chosen for the new Centurion tank in 1946. In this form, as a Meteor Mk 4B, the Meteor developed 650bhp at 2,250rpm. A dedicated engineering team based at the Acocks

The Meteor V12 tank engine was derived from the legendary Merlin aero engine. This example is a MkIII type for a late-model Cromwell tank, and was pictured on display at the Tank Museum in Bovington.

The Meteorite V8 was in turn a derivative of the Meteor V12. Though developed and built by Rover at Acocks Green, it usually wore Rolls-Royce identification. This example is one that had been converted to diesel by Ricardo.

The Thornycroft Antar (usually known as the Mighty Antar) was developed in the late 1940s around the Meteorite V8 engine. It was originally designed as an oilfield tractor unit for the Anglo-Iranian Oil Company but was later adopted by the British army as a tank transporter tractor.

Green plant developed further upgrades, and the final version of the Meteor (for the Conqueror tank in 1955) was the M120, which had 810bhp at 2,800rpm.

It was this Rover-managed engineering team at Acocks Green that designed and developed the Meteorite engine. This was a V8 derivative of the V12 Meteor with a smaller capacity of 18.01 litres, and shared its 60-degree vee configuration; both petrol and diesel versions were eventually manufactured. A V8 derivative of the Meteor was included in plans for experimental tanks as early as 1944, but the Meteorite became better known in 250bhp guise as the power plant of the Thornycroft Mighty Antar, a tractor unit intended for Middle East oilfield use. In the early 1950s the British Army adopted the Antar as a tank transporter tractor, and familiarity with the Meteorite engine led to its specification in at least one further tank project – a research vehicle built by Leyland in 1955–56 to enable FVRDE to test the layout of the proposed Chieftain MBT. In Mk 202B form for this tank, the Meteorite developed 520bhp at 2,700rpm.

The Centurion tank used a 650bhp version of the Meteor V12 engine that came from Rover's Acocks Green factory.

The final version of the Meteor engine had 810bhp and powered the 65-ton Conqueror heavy tank. This one was pictured in service with the British Army of the Rhine in 1962.

APPENDIX VI

Technical Specifications

TEN, TWELVE, FOURTEEN AND SIXTEEN (1946–1947) SPECIFICATIONS

Engine (Ten)
Four-cylinder with overhead valves
1389cc (66.5mm bore × 100mm stroke)
Compression ratio 5.9:1
Three main bearings
Single SU downdraught carburettor (to chassis 6110047); single Solex downdraught thereafter
44bhp at 4,200rpm

Engine (Twelve)
Four-cylinder with overhead valves
1496cc (69mm bore × 100mm stroke)
Compression ratio 5.7:1
Three main bearings
Single SU downdraught carburettor (to chassis 6210056); single Solex downdraught thereafter
48bhp at 4,200rpm

Engine (Fourteen)
Six-cylinder with overhead valves
1901cc (63.5mm bore × 100mm stroke)
Compression ratio 6.5:1
Four main bearings
Solex dual downdraught carburettor
55bhp at 4,200rpm

Engine (Sixteen)
Six-cylinder with overhead valves
2147cc (67.5mm bore × 100mm stroke)
Compression ratio 6.5:1
Four main bearings
Solex dual downdraught carburettor
60bhp at 4,200rpm

Gearbox
Four-speed with freewheel
Ratios: 3.4:1, 2.0:1, 1.5:1, 1.0:1

Axle ratio
4.7:1 (Sixteen)
4.88:1 (Ten, Twelve and Fourteen)

Steering
Burman Douglas worm-and-nut type

Suspension
Semi-elliptic leaf springs front and rear, with hydraulic piston-type dampers
Anti-roll bars front and rear on Twelve, Fourteen and Sixteen

Brakes
Girling rod-operated, with 12in drums

Wheel and tyre sizes
17in × 4.75 (Ten)
17in × 5.25 (Twelve)
17in × 5.50 (Fourteen and Sixteen)

Dimensions

Overall length	163in (4,140mm) Ten
	172in (4,369mm) Twelve
	175in (4,445mm) Fourteen and Sixteen
Wheelbase	105.5in (2,680mm) Ten
	112in (2,845mm) Twelve
	115in (2,921mm) Fourteen and Sixteen
Overall width	62in (1,575mm) Ten
	62.5in (1,587mm) Twelve, Fourteen and Sixteen
Overall height	61in (1,549mm) Twelve Sports Saloon
	62.25in (1,581mm) Fourteen and Sixteen Sports Saloon
	62.5in (1,587mm) Ten
	64in (1,626mm) Twelve Saloon
	65.25in (1,657mm) Fourteen and Sixteen Saloon
Track	51.5in (1,308mm) Ten
	54in (1,372mm) Twelve, Fourteen and Sixteen

Weights

2,794lb (1,270kg)	Ten
2,880lb (1,306kg)	Twelve Sports Saloon
2,910lb (1,320kg)	Twelve Saloon
3,097lb (1,405kg)	Fourteen and Sixteen Sports Saloon
3,135lb (1,422kg)	Fourteen and Sixteen Saloon

M MODEL SPECIFICATIONS, 1946

Engine
Four-cylinder with overhead inlet and side exhaust valves
699cc (57mm bore × 68.5mm stroke)
Compression ratio 9:1
(Probably) three main bearings
Single downdraught carburettor
28bhp at 5,000rpm

Gearbox
Four-speed, probably with synchromesh on 3rd and 4th speeds
Ratios 3.27:1, 2.05:1, 1.48:1, 1.00:1, reverse 3.64:1

Axle ratio
4.555:1

Steering
Worm and nut type

Suspension
Independent front suspension with swinging links, coil springs and hydraulic dampers
Rear axle with coil springs, radius arms, Panhard rod and hydraulic lever-arm dampers

Brakes
Girling Hydrastatic brakes with 8in drums

Wheel and tyre sizes
Pressed steel disc wheels with 14in diameter
4.75 × 14 tyres

Dimensions

Overall length	136in (3,454mm)
Wheelbase	77in (1,956mm)
Overall width	56in (1,422mm)
Overall height	55in (1,397mm)
Track	46in (1,168mm) front and rear

Weights
13.5cwt (686kg)

P3 60 AND 75 (1948–1949) SPECIFICATIONS

Engine (60)
Four-cylinder with overhead inlet and side exhaust valves
1595cc (69.5mm bore × 105mm stroke)
Compression ratio 7.1:1
Three main bearings
Solex 32PBI downdraught carburettor
60bhp at 4,000rpm (the *Automobile Engineer* for July 1948 shows the figures as 52bhp at 3,800rpm)

Engine (75)
Six-cylinder with overhead inlet and side exhaust valves
2103cc (65.2mm bore × 105mm stroke)
Compression ratio 7.25:1
Four main bearings
Solex 30PAA12 dual downdraught carburettor
72bhp at 4,000rpm

Gearbox
Four-speed with synchromesh on 3rd and 4th speeds, and freewheel
Ratios 3.37:1, 2.04:1, 1.48:1, 1.00:1, reverse 2.97:1

Axle ratio
4.7:1

Steering
Burman Douglas recirculating-ball type

Suspension
Independent front suspension with coil springs, anti-roll bar, and piston-type hydraulic dampers; telescopic dampers from approximately January 1949
Semi-elliptic rear springs with hydraulic telescopic dampers

Brakes
Girling brakes with hydraulic operation at the front and rod operation at the rear
12in drums all round

Wheel and tyre sizes
Pressed steel disc wheels with 17in diameter; 16in diameter optional
60: 5.25 × 17 tyres with 17in wheels, or 5.75 × 16 tyres with 16in wheels
75: 5.50 × 17 tyres with 17in wheels, or 5.75 × 16 tyres with 16in wheels

Dimensions

Overall length	171.25in (4,350mm)	
Wheelbase	110.5in (2,807mm)	
Overall width	63in (1,600mm)	
Overall height	65in (1,651mm)	Six-light body
	62in (1,575mm)	Four-light body
Track	51.187in (1,300mm) front	
	54.875in (1,394mm) rear	

Weights

60	2,968lb (1,346kg)	Six-light
60	2,940lb (1,334kg)	Four-light
75	3,108lb (1,410kg)	Six-light
75	3,080lb (1,397kg)	Four-light

LAND-ROVER (1948–53) SPECIFICATIONS

Engine (1948–51 models)
Four-cylinder with overhead inlet and side exhaust valves
1595cc (69.5mm bore × 105mm stroke)
Compression ratio 6.8:1
Three main bearings
Solex 32 PBI-2 carburettor
50bhp at 4,000rpm
80lb ft at 2,000rpm

Engine (1952–53 models)
Four-cylinder with overhead inlet and side exhaust valves
1997cc (77.8mm bore × 105mm stroke)
Compression ratio 6.8:1
Three main bearings
Solex 32 PBI-2 carburettor
52bhp at 4,000rpm
101lb ft at 1,500rpm

Gearbox
Permanent four-wheel drive with freewheel (1948–50 models); selectable four-wheel drive (1951–53 models)
Four-speed main gearbox with synchromesh on 3rd and 4th gears only; ratios 3.00:1, 2.04:1, 1.47:1, 1.00:1, reverse 2.54:1.
Two-speed transfer gearbox; ratios 1.148:1 (High) and 2.89:1 (Low)

Axle ratio
4.7:1 (first few hundred models with 4.88:1)

Steering
Recirculating-ball type with 15:1 ratio

Suspension
Semi-elliptic leaf springs all round with hydraulic telescopic dampers

Brakes
Girling drum brakes with hydraulic operation on all four wheels
10in × 1.5in drums all round
Separate 9in drum-type transmission parking brake operated by cable

Wheel and tyre sizes
Pressed steel disc wheels with 16in diameter
6.00 × 16 tyres standard; 7.00 × 16 optional; 6.50 × 16 on British military vehicles

Dimensions

Overall length	132in (3,353mm)
Wheelbase	80in (2,032mm)
Overall width	61in (1,549mm)
Unladen height	70.5in (1,971mm) with hood up
Track	50in (1,270mm)

Weights
2,594 lb (1,177kg)

P4 75 SPECIFICATIONS, 1949–53

Engine
Six-cylinder with overhead inlet and side exhaust valves
2103cc (65.2mm bore × 105mm stroke)
Compression ratio 7.25:1
Four main bearings
Two SU H4 carburettors
75bhp at 4,200rpm
111lb ft at 2,500rpm

Gearbox
Four-speed with synchromesh on 3rd and 4th speeds, and freewheel
Ratios 3.37:1, 2.04:1, 1.37:1, 1.00:1, reverse 2.97:1

Axle ratio
4.3:1

Steering
Burman Douglas recirculating-ball type with variable ratio

Suspension
Independent front suspension with wishbones, coil springs, telescopic dampers and anti-roll bar
Live rear axle with constant-rate semi-elliptic leaf springs and Panhard rod

Brakes
Girling brakes with hydraulic operation at the front and rod operation at the rear (1950 models); all-hydraulic operation (1951–53 models)
11in drums all round

Wheel and tyre sizes
Pressed steel disc wheels with 15in diameter and 4.5in rim
6.00 × 15 crossply tyres

Dimensions

Overall length	178.25in (4,527mm)
Wheelbase	111in (2,819mm)
Overall width	65.325in (1,659mm)
Overall height	63.25in (1,607mm)
Track	52in front (1,321mm)
	51.5in rear (1,308mm)

Weights

1950–51 models	3,108lb (1,410kg)
1952–53 models	3,200lb (1,451kg)

Index

First published in 2024 by
The Crowood Press Ltd
Ramsbury, Marlborough
Wiltshire SN8 2HR

enquiries@crowood.com
www.crowood.com

British Library Cataloguing-in-Publication Data
A catalogue record for this book is available from the British Library.

ISBN 978 0 7198 4412 6

The right of James Taylor to be identified as author of this work has been asserted by him in accordance with the Copyright, Designs and Patents Act 1988.

Acknowledgements

The information that underlies this book has come from more than four decades of research into the subject, and from countless individuals who have provided small pieces of the overall jigsaw. Many of those individuals have been former employees of the Rover Company, and it was always a privilege and a source of some personal excitement to be able to talk to them. Those whose memories had the most influence on the story in this book are all, sadly, no longer with us, but they deserve to be acknowledged here. My sincere thanks therefore go to Gordon Bashford, Arthur Goddard, Spen King, Tony Poole and Frank Shaw for providing information about these vital years at Rover. I am also pleased to acknowledge the immense and friendly help that has been provided by the archive staff at the British Motor Museum in Gaydon, where so many documents and photographs are now carefully stored.

Picture credits
Annand & Thompson/Alex Massey, p.83; Bache family, p.175; Gordon Bashford, p.15 (top, bottom left); J. Battersby, p.100; David Boar, p.170 (bottom); Eamonn Burnell, p.167 (all); Dirk Burrows, p.149; Creative Commons licence, p.33, p.36 (bottom), p.80, p.201 (top and bottom); Chris Dancey, p.40; Stephen C. Dickson, p.99; Peter Galilee, p.135; Nick Georgano/National Motor Museum, p.173 (bottom); Steve Glover, p.41 (top), p.75 (bottom), p.170 (top left and right); Harry Hilgerdenaar, p.43; Tobias Nordhausen, p.62; Tony Poole, p.139 (top); Robert Sargeant, p.133 (bottom left); Patrick Sutcliffe, p.126 (top); Jack Swaine/Ian Elliott, p.176; Swiss Car Register, p.87 (left); Paul Theys, p.134 (bottom left); Vauxford, p.191; Ken Watkin: 139 (bottom); Wilks family, p.108, 164 (all).

Typeset by Chennai Publishing Services

Cover design by Keith Wootton

Printed and bound in India by Nutech Print Services - India